*'God is closer to us than we could ever imagine
and loves us more than we could ever know.'*

This book is dedicated to my wife Pam,
who has always loved and believed in me
and for that I am and always will be truly grateful

Words of Life

The Parables of Jesus for People Today

Sean Loone

Michael Terence
Publishing

Foreword

As we listen to the words of Scripture during the course of the Church's Year, principally in the cycle of readings offered by the Lectionary, the Gospels in particular offer a distinctive insight into the person of Jesus Christ and his teachings. We learn about the life and death of Jesus, about the miracles he performed and the wonder of God that he reveals. Of all the ways that we learn about Jesus, it is perhaps the parables that he told that help to explore in greater depth our relationship with God the Father and the love and mercy that God so readily shares with the world through His Son, Jesus Christ.

The parables, through the gentle and sometimes challenging nature of ordinary and everyday life, reveal hidden and profound truths about the mystery of God and the experience of what it is to be human. In *Words of Life – The Parables of Jesus for People Today,'* Deacon Sean Loone seeks to explore the parables as a way of encountering God and deepening our relationship with him. Each of the three sections focuses on one of the Synoptic Gospels and the particular Gospel text given is followed by a reflection on its meaning relevant for people today and for their lives of faith.

As a fruit of his ministry of preaching Deacon Sean offers these insights in a style that is both readable and accessible. I am most grateful to Deacon Sean for his generosity in offering these prayerful reflections and for the way in which he enables the reader to encounter the presence of the living God through the rich teachings that the parables of Jesus continue to offer for our world today.

Bernard Longley
Archbishop of Birmingham

Preface

As a Roman Catholic Deacon my intention in writing this book is twofold, reflecting, at least in part, what I believe Christ has invited me to do for his people and the world. Firstly, I have written a book which is primarily about the scriptures and people, whereby I have invited the reader to understand just how close God is to each and every single one of us. To describe this, I have repeatedly used the phrase, *'closer to us than we could ever imagine and loving us more than we could ever know.'* This is my understanding of why Jesus came, to reveal how unconditionally and overwhelmingly we are all loved by God. The parables speak constantly of this love and how we are all surrounded by it every moment of our lives, we just fail to recognise it most of the time. This book then is my contribution to helping us all realise just how much we are loved by God. Deacons are called to be servants of the word, so this project is one way of exorcising my ministry and it is something I offer with all humility.

If you have read any of my three previous books you will know that I have donated all of the profits to charity. This also fits in well with my office as a Deacon because, as such, we are all called to be servants of charity. As a result, and, once again, I am donating all the profits from the sale of this book to a worthy cause. Jesus spent most of his time with the despised, unwanted, and rejected of the world. For this reason, I have chosen, *'The Catholic Association for Overseas Development'* (CAFOD) as the charity I am going to support with any profits made from the sale of this book. CAFOD do wonderful work with some of the poorest, most wretched and deprived people on earth and their philosophy fits in well with that of Pope Francis who calls on the church to have a *'preferential option for the poor.'* You can find out more about the work of CAFOD by going to, *cafod.org.uk.*

As I write these words, I find myself looking out at the world and am confronted with the reality of suffering humanity. I see the poor and the desperate in Afghanistan, children barely able to stand up in the Yemen and the innocent victims of aggression in the Ukraine to name but a few. My hope now is that the true potential for humanity can be seen in the pages of this book as revealed by Christ himself and that its profits may, somehow, make a contribution towards relieving the pain, misery and suffering of our fellow human beings.

Finally, and in conclusion, this project brings together two of the most important aspects of being a Deacon in the world today. That of being a servant of the word and a servant of charity. Putting it simply, servants-serve, and so the words of Jesus seem a fitting way to end this preface, *'I am among you as one who serves.'* (Luke 22:27)

Contents

Introduction

Dear Friends

It is always a humbling experience for me to sit down and write anything about God, which someone else may read and find helpful. My overwhelming motivation in writing this book is to simply deepen our relationship with Christ by reflecting on his word to the point that it impacts directly on the way in which we live. This particular work focuses on some of the parables told by Jesus, so let me begin by making clear what a parable is not. The parables are not simple stories with a moral message. To reduce them to such is, in fact, to fundamentally misrepresent what Jesus was aiming to do through them. Parables are stories told by Jesus but with a specific intent. Firstly, Jesus takes familiar things from everyday life that people would have seen all around them such as bread, wine, seeds, sheep, and shepherds and infuses them with mystical significance. The result of this is that the meaning of the parable itself is far more important than the content of each story. However, every parable that Jesus tells is also a revelation, which means that it reveals something about God and the Kingdom of Heaven as well as what it means to commit oneself to the loving service of others. For this reason, I like to use the symbol of the cross when talking about the parables whereby the upward beam points us towards God whilst the horizontal beam points us towards each other. As a result, whenever we explore any of the parables told by Jesus, we can automatically search for these two essential criteria.

One of the best ways I can describe the Bible is as God's love letter to humanity. When we were young, we had to be taught how to read and the same is true in later life when we come to sacred scripture. God is, of course, the supreme teacher and it is in and through his Son that God comes to find us. It is in Jesus Christ that we actually meet, face to face, as it were, the author of this letter. You see Jesus not only meets us in his words, but he actually lives them. The words of sacred scripture, therefore, prepare us to encounter Jesus in the midst of life as a living reality in the here and now. In other words, the parables of Jesus are dynamic because they trigger a reaction in us resulting in a response to both our understanding of God and the way in which he invites us to live our lives of faith today. Here it is vitally important to understand that God's word, including the parables, is given to all people because by its very nature, reflecting that of God, it is inclusive and not exclusive.

In Luke 5:4 Jesus tells Peter to *'Put out into deep water'* as he steps into his boat. It is a moment when grace invades Peter's life and what follows will change his life forever. The same is true for us as we read the words of life and encounter the living Lord through sacred scripture. Will we co-operate with him or not? Perhaps it is one of the most important decisions we will ever make. How exciting though, is that? Every time we read a parable of Jesus, we are having an encounter with the Lord of life who challenges us to follow him, just as he did with Peter all those centuries ago. Dare we read them in this way? Are we prepared to have our lives turned upside down? The parables are designed to change us. To change our understanding of what God is like and to change even the way in which we live our lives. In this way they challenge us to become ever more human and in doing so we become ever more like Christ himself. For this reason, I often think of reading the parables as a journey into our own faith as well as being a journey into our own humanity.

One of the major influences on my life and my understanding of God has been the documents of the Second Vatican Council. To this end, three Latin phrases come to mind the first of which is *'Lumen Gentium,'* meaning *'Light of the Nations.'* This is what the Church is called to be for all people as it proclaims the Gospel of Jesus Christ. Secondly, *'Gaudium et Spes,'* meaning *'Joy and Hope,'* this is what the Church is called live as it bears witness to the Gospel of Jesus Christ but again for all people. Finally, *'Dei Verbum,'* meaning *'Word of God'* which is, of course, what the parables are and define how the Church is called to live in the world today.

Christ, of course, stands at the heart of his Church because he is not only the light but the source of the light calling all people to holiness which is nothing less than an invitation to love God and our neighbour. The parables reveal these truths which is why they are so important to our lives of faith. In this short book I have tried to provide brief but meaningful reflections on many of them to help us understand not only what God is like but equally on how he invites us to live in relationship with him and each other. I have not written a reflection on every parable and have avoided repetition when they have appeared in more than one Gospel. To this end, I have followed a simple formula by choosing parables from each of the Synoptic Gospels, which are found in the three-year lectionary cycle observed, these days, by many churches.

Finally, a word on how I came to write this book. One Sunday after Mass, having preached on one of the parables, a parishioner came up to me and said, *'That should be the subject of your next book – the parables!'* To be honest, I smiled, nodded, and thought nothing of it but years later I began to realise that this was, in fact, exactly what God was inviting me to do. Then all of a sudden, I came to another conclusion that the whole process was like *'A mustard seed which, at the time of its sowing on earth, is the smallest of all the seeds. Yet once it is sown it grows up and becomes the biggest shrub of all.'* (Mark 4:31-32) Little did that parishioner, or I know, at the time, that they were planting a seed which would grow slowly and silently in my heart until, in God's own good time, it would take the form of this book.

The final few words of this introduction I am going to address to myself in the form of a question, *'Who am I to write a book such as this?'* My answer is, *'a nothing and a nobody,'* but in reading, praying, and reflecting on the parables, Christ has taught me, in fact, that this is more than enough. If I have learned anything personally, therefore, from completing this project and reflecting on the parables of Jesus for people today, it is that God is closer to us than we could ever imagine and loves us more than we could ever know.

I hope you will find reading this book helpful in deepening your relationship with Christ who is closer to us than we could ever imagine and loves us more than we could ever know. Please pay for me as I will for you.

God Bless

Sean

Part One:

Matthew

*'The kingdom of heaven is like treasure hidden in a field, which
someone found and hid; then in his joy he goes and sells
all that he has and buys that field.'
(Matthew 13:44)*

One:

The Sower

Matthew 13:1-23

'Open Minds and Soft Hearts'

That same day Jesus went out of the house and sat beside the sea. Such great crowds gathered around him that he got into a boat and sat there, while the whole crowd stood on the beach. And he told them many things in parables, saying: "Listen! A sower went out to sow. And as he sowed, some seeds fell on the path, and the birds came and ate them up. Other seeds fell on rocky ground, where they did not have much soil, and they sprang up quickly, since they had no depth of soil. But when the sun rose, they were scorched; and since they had no root, they withered away. Other seeds fell among thorns, and the thorns grew up and choked them. Other seeds fell on good soil and brought forth grain, some a hundredfold, some sixty, some thirty. Let anyone with ears listen!"

Then the disciples came and asked him, "Why do you speak to them in parables?" He answered, "To you it has been given to know the secrets of the kingdom of heaven, but to them it has not been given. For to those who have, more will be given, and they will have an abundance; but from those who have nothing, even what they have will be taken away. The reason I speak to them in parables is that 'seeing they do not perceive, and hearing they do not listen, nor do they understand.' With them indeed is fulfilled the prophecy of Isaiah that says: 'You will indeed listen, but never understand, and you will indeed look, but never perceive. For this people's heart has grown dull, and their ears are hard of hearing, and they have shut their eyes; so that they might not look with their eyes and listen with their ears and understand with their heart and turn and I would heal them.'

But blessed are your eyes, for they see, and your ears, for they hear. Truly I tell you, many prophets and righteous people longed to see what you see, but did not see it, and to hear what you hear, but did not hear it.

"Hear then the parable of the sower. When anyone hears the word of the kingdom and does not understand it, the evil one comes and snatches away what is sown in the heart; this is what was sown on the path. As for what was sown on rocky ground, this is the one who hears the word and

immediately receives it with joy; yet such a person has no root, but endures only for a while, and when trouble or persecution arises on account of the word, that person immediately falls away. As for what was sown among thorns, this is the one who hears the word, but the cares of the world and the lure of wealth choke the word, and it yields nothing. But as for what was sown on good soil, this is the one who hears the word and understands it, who indeed bears fruit and yields, in one case a hundredfold, in another sixty, and in another thirty."

If we are ever going to understand the meaning of the parables of Jesus then two things are essential from the start and these are,

- We need to have an open mind
- Our hearts must be soft

Without both of these we will never get anywhere near appreciating how the parables of Jesus reveal that the Kingdom of Heaven is, in fact, everywhere. So, as we begin our journey into understanding why and how the parables were such an important teaching method for Jesus Matthew makes a crucial point right at the beginning of our exploration. Jesus is the one who sows, his word, in the world. So, in our first parable of 'The Sower' Jesus occupies the role in these words: *'A sower went out to sow.'* Now the next point is vital if we are ever to really appreciate what Jesus is trying to reveal to us and it is this, in Jesus the Kingdom of God is perfectly realised. So, when Jesus tells a parable it becomes an invitation from him to live our lives in the same way that he did. So, our starting point always must be with Jesus himself. In other words, it is a necessary requirement to our understanding of what Jesus teaches to believe first who he is, which is nothing less than the Son of God. To any honest enquirer who struggles with this then an open mind and a soft heart makes for a good prerequisite.

Right, now let us press on with the parable. Jesus is the sower sowing God's word. Imagine at the time a farmer who has prepared his field and who now sets out with a bag of seeds over his shoulder. He takes a fist full of seeds out of the bag, walks across the ploughed land and throws his seed out in all directions.

It would have been a sight familiar to all those who had come to see and listen to Jesus. Jesus, however, is sowing the word of God, scattering it everywhere and inviting all those who hear it to respond. Yet there is something new and different going on when Jesus teaches. He offers people a challenge and invites them to live their lives in a different way and therefore to change or to be transformed. So, just as the seed, which will grow in the field symbolises new life so Jesus in and through his teaching also offers new life to all those who listen and understand.

However, if this is going to happen the old way of living, being and understanding must pass away. This is because Jesus is offering the words of life, a new way of being human, a new way of living and a new way of understanding God. Jesus, therefore, calls this *The Kingdom of Heaven*. Very few of us stop to think what it means to be a human being but Jesus in and through his life and ministry will do just that. We have already said that in Jesus the Kingdom of God is fully realised. To be one of his followers means a complete transformation in our understanding of what it means to be human, and he will teach us how to do it, but we have to be prepared to change. Our old way of thinking and acting must be transformed. Or putting it another way our old self has to die so that our new and true self can be transformed in and through our faith in Christ. This is the invitation that Jesus offers to all those who would truly listen to him. However, it is also a call to engagement with the world, to be part of his mission, which believe it or not is to make the world more human.

The actual message of Jesus heads straight for our hearts, plummeting the depths of our being by feeding our souls. It is only there that we can ever truly listen to the words of Jesus and recognise them for what they are, the words of life. Listening and indeed hearing by themselves can never be enough without our hearts having been touched. This is why the first point that I made was that if we are ever going to understand the meaning of the parables then we must have soft hearts, which are open to the word of God. Only then will his words penetrate our inner most being and transform our lives. Followers of Jesus and his body on earth the church must have open hearts, sensitive to what only God can teach us. If this is not the case then we will never know what it is like to experience the power of God, through his grace, to transform our lives.

Now getting back to the parable itself. One of the points I would like to make is to notice how Jesus includes everyone and excludes no one. To this end, he scatters the seed everywhere, how we react is up to us. If our minds are closed and our hearts are hardened, then we might listen to and hear the words of Jesus, but they fail to penetrate our inner most being. These are like the seeds, which fall along the path. If on the other hand we take the time to stop, listen and reflect something does happen. Here our minds are open and our hearts soft; we are sensitive to and willingly co-operating with God's grace at work in our lives. Now understanding comes and we are drawn ever closer to the Kingdom of Heaven. Putting it another way we are becoming more like Christ and therefore more human. As this happens our understanding of God's plan, in and through his son, is also deepened.

Some people, however, although invited by Christ keep their minds closed and their hearts hardened. As a result, they fail to understand the true message of Jesus and so it has no impact on their lives whatsoever. Such hard or closed hearts in particular means that the word of God, as sown by Jesus, fails to have any effect on the way in which life is lived. This, in fact, acts as a wakeup call to all those who would call themselves Christian today. We have ears but do we truly listen, and we have eyes, but do we really see? Are our hearts open to the word of God to the point that our very souls are touched by his word? Perhaps the true test is to, once again, look at our own humanity and be brave enough to compare it to the life lived by Jesus himself. Are we willing to pledge our lives to him? Are we willing to be part of his transforming grace to change the world and so make it more human? This whole process starts with our own hearts and our own lives of faith. In essence, the call by Jesus to follow him and the invitation to listen to his word is nothing less than God asking us to join our lives with his by identifying who we are with his Kingdom. In truth, this is a call to be different but not in a superior way but in a way which leads to becoming more like Christ and therefore more human. Ultimately the parable of *'The Sower'* invites us to see, believe and understand that we can live our lives according to the Kingdom of Heaven in the here and now, but this must be clearly visible to a world with increasingly closed minds and hard hearts.

Two:

Leaven

Matthew 13:24-43

'We Have a Problem!'

He put before them another parable: "The kingdom of heaven may be compared to someone who sowed good seed in his field; but while everybody was asleep, an enemy came and sowed weeds among the wheat, and then went away. So, when the plants came up and bore grain, then the weeds appeared as well. And the slaves of the householder came and said to him, 'Master, did you not sow good seed in your field? Where, then, did these weeds come from?' He answered, 'An enemy has done this.' The slaves said to him, 'Then do you want us to go and gather them?' But he replied, 'No; for in gathering the weeds you would uproot the wheat along with them. Let both of them grow together until the harvest; and at harvest time I will tell the reapers, Collect the weeds first and bind them in bundles to be burned, but gather the wheat into my barn.'"

He put before them another parable: "The kingdom of heaven is like a mustard seed that someone took and sowed in his field; it is the smallest of all the seeds, but when it has grown it is the greatest of shrubs and becomes a tree, so that the birds of the air come and make nests in its branches."

He told them another parable: "The kingdom of heaven is like yeast that a woman took and mixed in with three measures of flour until all of it was leavened."

Jesus told the crowds all these things in parables; without a parable he told them nothing. This was to fulfil what had been spoken through the prophet: "I will open my mouth to speak in parables; I will proclaim what has been hidden from the foundation of the world."

Then he left the crowds and went into the house. And his disciples approached him, saying, "Explain to us the parable of the weeds of the field." He answered, "The one who sows the good seed is the Son of Man; the field is the world, and the good seed are the children of the kingdom; the weeds are the children of the evil one, and the enemy who sowed them is the devil; the harvest is the end of the age, and the reapers are angels. Just as the weeds are collected and burned up with fire, so will it be at the end of the age. The Son of Man will send his angels, and they will collect out of his kingdom all causes of sin and all evildoers, and they will throw them into the furnace of fire, where there will be weeping and gnashing of teeth. Then the righteous will shine like the sun in the kingdom of their Father. Let anyone with ears listen!

Right so here is the problem, how do you convince people that the Kingdom of Heaven is everywhere? It was a problem for Jesus over 2,000 years ago just as it remains a problem for his followers today. The main issue then, just as it is now, seems to be that people are either looking in the wrong place or looking for the wrong thing. So as the well-known saying goes, *'We have a problem!'* At the time of Jesus people had been brought up to expect the spectacular in relation to God and, perhaps, most people have the same expectations today; after all is God not supposed to be all knowing, all present and all powerful?

Jesus on the other hand wanted to reveal the God who is in the here and now or as we might say in the ordinary events and things of everyday life. This is why Jesus told parables featuring items and situations that people were familiar with and infused them with the life of God; think about seed, oil, bread, vines, water, sheep, and shepherds to name but a few. You see in Jesus himself the Kingdom of God was actually present before their very eyes that is why he was able to teach the people with authority. However, Jesus also wanted the people to see something else that if only we could realise the Kingdom was here in the midst of our lives now, then surely everything would change.

So, Jesus, as we do today, faced a challenge, to help people understand not only who he was and is but also how it is possible to perceive the Kingdom of God in our lives as a living reality in the here and now.

Is it possible to shift peoples' attention away from the spectacular and find God in the ordinary? To discover, in fact, that the Kingdom of Heaven is everywhere? When he was a young boy growing up in Nazareth Jesus would have been familiar with a sight, which took place very early in the morning on the eve of every Sabbath. Rising at first light Mary, his mother, along with a group of other women would have gathered together on a kind of patio area in order to prepare the bread for the week ahead. Part of that role, performed by the women, was to place the leaven in the bread so that it would rise. Only a small amount was needed but without it the bread would not rise and remain flat. In many ways Jesus here was talking about how God acts like a mother by placing his leaven in the world.

Jesus therefore is encouraging the people to see the Kingdom of God acting in the same way as the leaven in the bread. So, just like a woman or his mother placing a tiny amount of leaven inside the bread so that it might rise, this is also how God acts. We need to pause at this point and really attempt to take in the enormity of what Jesus is actually saying in this parable and the key to our understanding is, of course, the leaven. The leaven is placed inside the bread; obvious I know but see what happens when we apply this to God. God acts in the same way. Think of it like this, God never imposes his will from the outside, it is the mighty and the powerful that act like that. Rather Jesus is telling us that God operates from within in a silent and hidden way. So do not look for the great and the spectacular in relation to God but rather for the ordinary and you might just discover that the Kingdom of Heaven is everywhere.

In this way Jesus is transforming our understanding of what God is actually like. You see the truth is that God does not seek to coerce, manipulate, dominate, or control us. It is we who are quite good at that. Rather God seeks simply to attract or seduce us. This results in a completely different way of understanding God and if we can, in some way, comprehend this then it leads to our own transformation.

So, when we apply this to our own lives of faith this is how it works. Jesus, therefore, is inviting us to be the leaven by continuing his transforming work but to do this our lives must reflect his. The starting point always must be with humility and love but equally the vocation of the Christian is to bear witness to both justice and the truth. However, we should have nothing to do whatsoever with domination or control because all this does is place us on the outside of people's lives. Remember that manipulation, coercion, domination, power, and control have nothing to do with the Kingdom of God as revealed by Jesus Christ.

Instead, we need to place ourselves in the midst of people's lives sharing all their ups and downs and offering ourselves in humble service as followers of Jesus. In this way, just like that leaven, we are working from the inside sharing the struggles, hopes and fears of all our brothers and sisters. Yet we are able to offer something, which is our faith, transformed lives, changed by our belief in Jesus Christ. Here then we have the heart of what Jesus was and continues to say to all those who would follow him. It is through living lives of humble service, transformed by our love of Jesus, that we become more like him and therefore more human. Living such lives from within the communities in which we live enables us to become the leaven of God in the world, small and insignificant in one sense but with the power to transform humanity in another.

Three:

Treasure

Mathew 13:44-52

'Time to Choose'

"The kingdom of heaven is like treasure hidden in a field, which someone found and hid; then in his joy he goes and sells all that he has and buys that field.

"Again, the kingdom of heaven is like a merchant in search of fine pearls; on finding one pearl of great value, he went and sold all that he had and bought it.

"Again, the kingdom of heaven is like a net that was thrown into the sea and caught fish of every kind; when it was full, they drew it ashore, sat down, and put the good into baskets but threw out the bad. So, it will be at the end of the age. The angels will come out and separate the evil from the righteous and throw them into the furnace of fire, where there will be weeping and gnashing of teeth.

"Have you understood all this?" They answered, "Yes." And he said to them, "Therefore every scribe who has been trained for the kingdom of heaven is like the master of a household who brings out of his treasure what is new and what is old."

The first point I would make here is that believing in Jesus, in one sense over the millennia, has not changed, in so far as, it is not easy. If we go back 2,000 years some people, as we know, were attracted by Jesus whilst others either doubted or quite simply rejected him. In that sense nothing has changed. Yet the choice and it is important to make that point remains, do we believe in and follow him, or do we live our lives as if he never really existed? In a world which seems to promote individual importance and happiness over and above that of others the choice is a contrasting one. To follow Jesus is nothing less than a commitment to making the world in which we live a better place for all people. However, to achieve this we also need to be aware of what it means to be a human being, which is, in fact, something Jesus invites us to participate in. This is because to follow him involves a commitment to living our humanity to the fullest extent possible, however, we do not do this for ourselves but for others. To look into the face of Jesus is to see and recognise not only the Son of God but our human potential and if we accept his invitation to, *'Come and follow me,'* (Matthew 4: 18-20) then our lives can never be the same again. If this is ever going to happen though we must be prepared for our hearts to be touched by his grace and this is something Jesus knew all too well as he taught the people using parables.

So, in this passage we have, in effect, no less than two parables. In them Jesus asks his audience to imagine a poor worker about his daily task digging in a field which does not belong to him. Then all of a sudden and completely unexpectedly he finds some hidden treasure. This would have been something beyond his wildest dreams and his heart must have leapt with both shock and surprise. Immediately and this is an important word because he has no hesitation whatsoever, he goes off, sells everything he has to buy the field and so possess the treasure.

Now when we turn, this time, to the wealthy merchant, note the contrast in the status of the two men by the way, dealing in fine pearls. He finds the one pearl, which makes all the rest he has pale into insignificance by comparison. So, what does he do? In fact, just like the previous poor farmer, there is absolutely no hesitation at all. He sells all the pearls he has just to purchase that one pearl. As a result, he can now go off, just like the poor farmer, a happy man.

So, here is the big question, *'what does it all mean?'*

Well first and foremost Jesus tells us what the parable is actually about by beginning with the words, *'The Kingdom of Heaven is like ………'* Hence, we know the parables are about the Kingdom of Heaven, yet we also know it is hidden. How true this is when we think about the number of people in the world today who do not believe in Jesus. If they do not believe in Jesus, then how can they believe in his mission? As I said earlier to believe in and follow

Jesus is to accept an invitation to maximise our human potential but how is this possible if we do not, in fact, know him? The simple truth though is that all is revealed in the life and message of Jesus himself. Once again everything must point to Jesus because he is both the source and the origin of what it really means to be human. To be truly alive any Christian community must accept and embrace this simple truth.

To discover that Jesus is the source and origin of everything and thus gives true meaning to human life and existence must lead to transformation. That is to say, it must change the life of the one who discovers and believes it forever. Hence Jesus uses the word, *'joy'* to describe those who discover this truth for themselves, about the Kingdom of Heaven. Such a person, has in reality, discovered the meaning of life, and now has something on which to base their whole existence; Jesus himself. For this reason, the church, in whatever form it takes, must be a place of joy.

Note that the two contrasting individuals in the parables both make the same choice by selling all that they have. You see for them; nothing can be more important than the Kingdom of Heaven and what it brings. In contrast everything by comparison seems less important and here also lies the challenge. What exists in our lives and in the life of the church which appears to have a disproportionate importance compared to the Kingdom of Heaven? What do we and the church need to lose if we are to rediscover the truth that Jesus is, in fact, everything? How much of our time and that of our church is taken up with those things which in reality do not proclaim the Gospel of truth and life? How much of our positive energy is consumed by issues which are, in effect, not important? Perhaps what Jesus is suggesting in these parables is the need for a stripping away of anything that we have attached importance to which prevents us from recognising him. It takes both bravery and courage for the church to strip back all those things, which in many ways have been comforting, in order to find that behind them, is nothing less than the face of Christ himself.

Four:

Forgiveness

Matthew 18:21-35

'The Trap!'

Then Peter came and said to him, "Lord, if another member of the church sins against me, how often should I forgive? As many as seven times?" Jesus said to him, "Not seven times, but I tell you, seventy-seven times.

"For this reason, the kingdom of heaven may be compared to a king who wished to settle accounts with his slaves. When he began the reckoning, one who owed him ten thousand talents was brought to him; and, as he could not pay, his lord ordered him to be sold, together with his wife and children and all his possessions, and payment to be made. So, the slave fell on his knees before him, saying, 'Have patience with me, and I will pay you everything.' And out of pity for him, the lord of that slave released him and forgave him the debt. But that same slave, as he went out, came upon one of his fellow slaves who owed him a hundred denarii; and seizing him by the throat, he said, 'Pay what you owe.' Then his fellow slave fell down and pleaded with him, 'Have patience with me, and I will pay you.' But he refused; then he went and threw him into prison until he would pay the debt. When his fellow slaves saw what had happened, they were greatly distressed, and they went and reported to their lord all that had taken place. Then, his lord summoned him and said to him, 'You wicked slave! I forgave you all that debt because you pleaded with me. Should you not have had mercy on your fellow slave, as I had mercy on you?' And in anger his lord handed him over to be tortured until he would pay his entire debt. So, my heavenly Father will also do to every one of you, if you do not forgive your brother or sister from your heart."

When Jesus tells a parable about forgiveness, what do we expect? Forgiveness, right? Well take your time and read the parable through again focusing on how it ends. Shockingly it actually ends without forgiveness, so we are entitled to ask, what exactly is going on?

To begin with let us start with the opening paragraph with Peter asking Jesus, *'Lord how many times shall I forgive my brother when he sins against me? Up to seven times?'* Jesus answered, *'I tell you, not seven times, but seventy-seven times.'* Now this, of course, is what we expect. For the Jew seven is, in fact, a perfect number so to forgive someone seven times amounts to perfect forgiveness. Yet Jesus takes this even further when he insists on forgiving those who wrong us up to seventy-seven times! We are, of course, all used to the God of forgiveness being revealed through the life, death and resurrection of his son, Jesus Christ and this is exactly what appears to be going on here. Yet a closer examination of the parable does not support this or does it? You see there is a *'trap'* waiting for us here and we need to tread very carefully if we are to truly understand what Jesus is trying to teach us about forgiveness.

Right so let us spend a little time, first of all, examining the parable. Things start off really well with a King forgiving one of his servants a huge debt that would be impossible for him to repay. Jesus often does this in his parables, here by exaggerating the amount of the debt he is drawing our attention to God's overwhelming capacity to forgive us, no matter what we have done. Or putting it another way there is nothing we can do that will separate us from the love of God and his forgiveness. However, the same servant refuses to forgive a fellow servant who owes him an insignificantly small amount. In fact, he has him thrown in prison until all the debt is repaid. When the King hears about it, he is absolutely furious, summons the servant who owed him the huge amount and tells him off for his lack of mercy to a fellow servant. He then has him thrown in prison until the debt is paid, which, of course, we all know is impossible.

At this point we think we know the meaning of the parable and this where we fall into the *'trap.'* If the King is God and he forgives the original servant then we should be like him and forgive each other. We should not, however, be like the servant who failed to forgive his fellow servant. It is as simple as that or is it because here lies the *'trap.'* You see the parable begins so positively with Jesus telling us we must forgive as many as seventy-seven times or putting it another way we must always forgive. Yet if the King does represent God then the parable does not end with forgiveness but with eternal punishment. So, this leaves us with the question, what is going on and what is Jesus trying to teach us about forgiveness today?

To answer this question successfully requires us to be honest with ourselves. In my own reflections on what it means to be a follower of Jesus I always make the point that he invites us to become more human as a result of putting into practice, in our own lives, his teachings. This involves something new, a different way of being, a fresh way of approaching life, seeing the world through the eyes of faith. Yet very often, we are dragged back into what many might call the reality of the world. Hence part of us believes that the world would be a better place if everything was based on a strict set of enforceable rules, which would make sure those who do not conform are punished. However, does such a world have any real place for forgiveness of the kind Jesus teaches and if it does not, then what kind of humanity is the result? Taking it even further, if God does not, in fact, forgive, then what does that mean ultimately for us?

If we are brutally honest with ourselves the truth of the matter is that not to forgive has become the norm. Indeed, in some cases it is seen as the right course of action where there has been humiliation or a great act of injustice. Imagine that, relegating one of the central teachings of Jesus to a level well below that which he himself placed on it. If this is the case, how then can the world ever become more human? If we deny the centrality of compassion and forgiveness in the ministry of Jesus and fail to incorporate it into our lives of faith then, in truth, what have we become?

Right so how can we make sense out of a parable told by Jesus himself which appears to deny the ultimate centrality of forgiveness in his teaching? All of us fall into the *'trap,'* do we not, of believing that the least thing the servant can do is forgive his fellow servant who owed him so little? Yet compare this to what the King actually did at the beginning of the parable forgiving the same servant such a huge debt, one impossible to repay. This is what God's forgiveness is like and this is the point made by Jesus. Going back to the opening conversation with Peter Jesus, in effect, normalises forgiveness. Putting it another way, forgiveness is not something extraordinary but a natural consequence of believing in God and following his son, Jesus. The point Jesus is making is that we, in fact, live every moment and every second of our lives sustained by the mercy, compassion, forgiveness and love of God. What should be the least thing we must do in response to that? The answer is simple, forgive.

Five:

Love

Matthew 20:1-16

'Time for a Revolution'

"For the kingdom of heaven is like a landowner who went out early in the morning to hire labourers for his vineyard. After agreeing with the labourers for the usual daily wage, he sent them into his vineyard. When he went out about nine o'clock, he saw others standing idle in the marketplace; and he said to them, 'You also go into the vineyard, and I will pay you whatever is right.' So, they went. When he went out again about noon and about three o'clock, he did the same. And about five o'clock he went out and found others standing around; and he said to them, 'Why are you standing here idle all day?' They said to him, 'Because no one has hired us.' He said to them, 'You also go into the vineyard.' When evening came, the owner of the vineyard said to his manager, 'Call the labourers and give them their pay, beginning with the last and then going to the first.' When those hired about five o'clock came, each of them received the usual daily wage. Now when the first came, they thought they would receive more; but each of them also received the usual daily wage. And when they received it, they grumbled against the landowner, saying, 'These last worked only one hour, and you have made them equal to us who have borne the burden of the day and the scorching heat.' But he replied to one of them, 'Friend, I am doing you no wrong; did you not agree with me for the usual daily wage? Take what belongs to you and go; I choose to give to this last the same as I give to you. Am I not allowed to do what I choose with what belongs to me? Or are you envious because I am generous?' So, the last will be first, and the first will be last."

I have always been inspired by the words of the Prophet Isaiah who when talking about God said, *'For my thoughts are not your thoughts, neither are your ways my ways, declares the Lord.'* (Isaiah 55: 8-9) For me this makes something abundantly clear that if we are, in any way, to understand what God is like and how he invites us to live then we must think and act in a completely different way. Remember that line from the Lord's Prayer, *'Your will be done?'*

Not my will but God's will! Now it is time to find out what this means, and Jesus makes something shockingly clear in the parable of the labourers in the vineyard.

I think it is true to say that none of us like to be treated unfairly or unjustly. It irritates us and puts our back up. The world should not be like that, surely there are rules of behaviour, a code of conduct, which makes it clear that all people should be treated equally and fairly. After all, is this not obvious to any decent and right-minded person? Right, now I have got that off my chest let us have a look at the parable and what Jesus and therefore God is trying to teach about himself and how he invites us to live.

The scene is probably autumn and it is time to harvest the grapes. In the village or town square there are groups of men who do not own their own land and so are waiting to be hired. As Jesus tells the parable with the people gathered around him, we are left with the question, how will he reveal to them the outrageous nature of God's universal and unconditional love through this simple story?

The parable itself, beautiful in its simplicity, is quite remarkable in the way in which it challenges our sense of right and wrong. The owner of a vineyard hires the poor workers he finds in the square to harvest his grapes. However, he does so at different hours of the day including the eleventh hour. When the work is done at the end of the day, he pays each of the workers the same, the sum they had all agreed, one silver coin; enough for a family to live on.

Now the problems start because the workers hired at the beginning of the day are not happy that those employed at the end are paid the same as them. Putting it in their own words they are not happy because the owner of the vineyard has treated all the workers equally.

Now I wonder how we would feel if having worked a long, hard day in the hot baking sun we were paid exactly the same as those who had only worked one hour. It somehow just does not feel right, it is not fair surely; or we might even say it is simply wrong! At this point listen to the reply of the owner of the vineyard, *'Are you envious because I am generous?'*

So, what is really going on here, what is Jesus really trying to tell us? Could it be that the message is so outrageously revolutionary that even after all these centuries we are still not ready to accept it? Part of us wants to scream out that surely those who have worked more deserve more. Good works deserve recognition, do they not? How can God be good to those people who, let us be honest, have done very little to earn it? Are there no privileges for those who have dedicated their whole lives to good works? It is at this point that we need to return to the words of the Prophet Isaiah, *'For my thoughts are not your thoughts, neither are your ways my ways, declares the Lord.'* (Isaiah 55: 8-9)

You see what Jesus confronts us with here is nothing less than the unconditional and overwhelming love of God, which throws all our sense of right and wrong out of the window. It is outrageous and revolutionary at the same time and that is why it literally shocks us. For God loves all people equally, reflected in the silver coin given to each of the workers, no matter how long they had laboured in the vineyard. This pulls us back into allowing God to be God and as result challenges us to the very core of our being. God's love is infinite and given to whom he chooses simply because that is the expression of his overwhelming generosity. We are tempted to say, given our limitations, surely there are people who do not deserve God's love? Or putting it another way, you should get from God what you deserve. The Prophet Isaiah though reminds us, as does the Lord's Prayer, that God is not like that because he is not like us. God only knows how to love, and that love includes all those we describe as not deserving of it.

The parable is, therefore, a challenge to us all. It reveals what God's love is actually like and leaves us with these simple words of invitation, *'Go, and do the same yourself.'* (Luke 10:37)

Six:

Action

Matthew 21:28-32

'Actions speak louder than words'

"What do you think? A man had two sons; he went to the first and said, 'Son, go and work in the vineyard today.' He answered, 'I will not'; but later he changed his mind and went. The father went to the second and said the same; and he answered, 'I go, sir'; but he did not go. Which, of the two did the will of his father?" They said, "The first." Jesus said to them, "Truly I tell you; the tax collectors and the prostitutes are going into the kingdom of God ahead of you. For John came to you in the way of righteousness and you did not believe him, but the tax collectors and the prostitutes believed him; and even after you saw it, you did not change your minds and believe him.

For a long time, this parable troubled me. It seems so simple and the minute I think I know what it means the meaning escapes me. Then one day I had a breakthrough and discovered that the parable is, in fact, aimed primarily at the religious leaders of the day. Jesus is approaching the temple when he is stopped and questioned by the chief priests and elders about his authority. In response to their harassment Jesus tells them the parable.

The story itself is quite simple with a father asking his two sons to go and work in the vineyard for him. The first tells him straight, *'I will not go!'* But after a while changes his mind and does as his father requests by going to work in the vineyard. The second on the other hand answers enthusiastically, *'I will go.'* But of course, he really has no intention of doing anything of the kind.

Now at first sight the meaning, of which even the religious leaders agree, is that *'actions speak louder than words.'* Or putting it another way, God emphasises the importance of deeds over talk. The way we live our lives of faith has priority over just talking about it. So, is there more to the parable or is that it?

We only find this parable in Matthew and that is part of the key to understanding its meaning. There is no escaping the truth that in this parable Jesus is quite harsh but remember to whom it is addressed, the religious leaders of the day. Now listen again to what he says directly to them, *'I tell you the truth, the tax collectors and the prostitutes are entering the kingdom of God ahead of you.'*

We now need to unpack this a little further to see what it really means. On the one hand the religious leaders have said *'Yes'* to God and proceed to teach and preach his Law. However, when Jesus confronts them with his message and with his authority, which comes directly from God and challenges them to seek the kingdom of righteousness, they reject him. Thus, by denying Jesus they are, in reality, saying *'No,'* to God.

Now let us turn our attention to the tax collectors and prostitutes mentioned by Jesus in the parable. According to the religious leaders of the day such people were sinners, condemned by their own actions and therefore rejected by God. In other words, they have said *'No'* to God and remain beyond both the Law and the temple. Yet this same people have embraced both Jesus and his message. Indeed, Jesus is surrounded by those condemned by the religious leaders of the day. Think about Matthew, a tax collector himself and Zacchaeus, the poor, the sick, the lame, the prostitutes and all those marginalised and separated out by the chief priests and elders. All these people flock to Jesus and accept his proclamation of the Kingdom of God, which in effect means they are really saying *'Yes,'* when they had been labelled as saying *'No!'* Such people in fact embraced Jesus as the one sent from the father who teaches them not only with authority but perhaps more importantly with love. Little wonder then, that Jesus has such harsh words for all religious leaders both then and now who would put any stumbling block between him and those who seek the mercy, compassion, love, and forgiveness offered to them by God. For it is in such seeking that action is to be found and did we not say right that the beginning that, *'actions speak louder than words.'*

Seven:

The Tenants and the Vineyard

Mathew 21:33-43

'Outrageous'

"Listen to another parable. There was a landowner who planted a vineyard, put a fence around it, dug a wine press in it, and built a watchtower. Then he leased it to tenants and went to another country. When the harvest time had come, he sent his slaves to the tenants to collect his produce. But the tenants seized his slaves and beat one, killed another, and stoned another. Again, he sent other slaves, more than the first; and they treated them in the same way. Finally, he sent his son to them, saying, 'They will respect my son.' But when the tenants saw the son, they said to themselves, 'This is the heir; come, let us kill him and get his inheritance.' So, they seized him, threw him out of the vineyard, and killed him. Now when the owner of the vineyard comes, what will he do to those tenants?" They said to him, "He will put those wretches to a miserable death and lease the vineyard to other tenants who will give him the produce at the harvest time."

Jesus said to them, "Have you never read in the scriptures, 'The stone that the builders rejected has become the cornerstone; this was the Lord's doing, and it is amazing in our eyes'?

Therefore, I tell you, the kingdom of God will be taken away from you and given to a people that produces the fruits of the kingdom.

The problem with parables is that we tend to apply them to the world of 2,000 years ago when they are, in fact, nothing less than the words of life itself and contain eternal truths. This means that they are life-giving and timeless. As a result, they are just as applicable to us and the way in which we live our lives of faith today, as they were to the people who heard them for the first time directly from Jesus himself. This is something that we should never forget even when the message hits home hard.

When we look at the parable of *'The Tenants in the Vineyard,'* it is extremely important to recognise just how hard-hitting it really is.

However, although Jesus is primarily addressing the religious leaders of the day his message is equally applicable to all those, including us, who would follow him today.

The premise itself is quite simple. A man rents out his vineyard to tenants who at harvest time refuse to hand over the agreed produce. As a result, the owner is deprived of the fruit which rightfully belonged to him. As the owner sends servant after servant to collect the harvest, each time they are either beaten, stoned, or killed. In the end the owner sends his own son believing that now, surely, there can be no misunderstanding. Yet the response is the same, they throw him out of the vineyard and put him to death. Perhaps now it is the tenants who are thinking, *'Surely the owner will understand that this vineyard does, in fact, belong to us!'*

Now let us return to Jesus as he tells this parable to the religious of the day and asks the question, *'When the owner comes what will he do to those tenants?'* At this point, the religious leaders are forced to come to a terrible conclusion of their own, *'He will bring those wretches to a wretched end and will rent the vineyard to other tenants, who will give him his share of the crop at harvest time.'* In so doing did they really recognise that they were, in fact, condemning themselves? Jesus, however, removes any element of confusion which might be lingering in their minds when he replies, *'Therefore I tell you that the Kingdom of God will be taken away from you and given to a people who will produce its fruit.'*

At this moment it might be a good idea to take a breath before proceeding because now we have the task of applying this to our own lives of faith and this process will not be easy and quite rightly so. The first point to make is that the tenants are unworthy for two reasons. Firstly, they fail to recognise the son and secondly, they do this because they identified themselves as the owners of the vineyard. Or putting it another way, the religious leaders of the day had replaced God with themselves, refused to recognise the identity and authority of Jesus and claimed that they were nothing less than the masters of the people of God.

So, what does this mean for us and those who claim to be

followers of Jesus today? God demands fruit but it must be worthy of his Kingdom. To identify yourself with Jesus is to identify yourself with the God of mercy, compassion, forgiveness, and love. This is the fruit demanded by God and proclaimed by his son through the parables we are exploring in this project. It is a way of life projected outwards to all those in need, including all people and excluding no one. It is seen through tenderness and love lived out in lives practically engaged in helping the poor, disadvantaged, hopeless and helpless. It is to be seen in those serving and loving those found on the margins of life and at its heart is Jesus, the Son of God, who is to be recognised, served, and loved in all those who suffer.

To those church leaders, today, who fail to recognise this then the message is abundantly clear, *'The Kingdom will be taken away from you and given to a people who will produce its fruit.'* The parable makes it crystal clear, therefore, that the people belong to God and that God invites them to come to him. No one has the power or authority to prevent this from happening, but we all have the responsibility to bring it to fruition.

Eight:

The Banquet

Matthew 22:1-14

'The Great Invitation'

Once more Jesus spoke to them in parables, saying: "The kingdom of heaven may be compared to a king who gave a wedding banquet for his son. He sent his slaves to call those who had been invited to the wedding banquet, but they would not come. Again, he sent other slaves, saying, 'Tell those who have been invited: Look, I have prepared my dinner, my oxen and my fat calves have been slaughtered, and everything is ready; come to the wedding banquet.' But they made light of it and went away, one to his farm, another to his business, while the rest seized his slaves, mistreated them, and killed them. The king was enraged. He sent his troops, destroyed those murderers, and burned their city. Then he said to his slaves, 'The wedding is ready, but those invited were not worthy. Go therefore into the main streets, and invite everyone you find to the wedding banquet.' Those slaves went out into the streets and gathered all whom they found, both good and bad; so, the wedding hall was filled with guests.

"But when the king came in to see the guests, he noticed a man there who was not wearing a wedding robe, and he said to him, 'Friend, how did you get in here without a wedding robe?' And he was speechless. Then the king said to the attendants, 'Bind him hand and foot, and throw him into the outer darkness, where there will be weeping and gnashing of teeth.' For many are called, but few are chosen."

In my parish church of *Our Lady of the Wayside* there stands a statue of the Risen Lord with arms open wide in a gesture of welcome to all people. Inscribed into the stone of the altar are the words, *'I will pour out my spirit on all flesh.'* For me there can be no ambiguity in these words and symbols because their meaning is both simple and obvious that God, through his son, invites all people to him. Or putting it another way Jesus, himself, is the invitation to the Father. This is what comes to mind as I reflect on the meaning and significance of this parable. Once again, Jesus sets about revealing the nature and being of God set against the background of our response to him.

Jesus is of course filled with the Spirit of his Father to the point that it literally overflows from him so that everything he says and does reflects God's overwhelming and unconditional love for all people. Growing up in Nazareth Jesus would have been all too familiar with the hard life most people had to live there. For them feast days, weddings and of course the Sabbath were all a relief from the grind of day-to-day living. When such festivals came around the poor would have the opportunity to enjoy life, taking a break from just surviving. The mere suggestion of being invited to a banquet with all their friends and relatives would have filled their hearts with pure joy.

With this in mind Jesus, offers them a vision of what God has in store for them, nothing less than a marvellous banquet to which everyone is invited. Yet Jesus takes even this a stage further by making it clear that he, himself is the invitation. Throughout his ministry Jesus sits down with tax collectors, the unwanted, the rejected, the despised and the unloved and eats with them. Now he makes it clear how this will be the case at the end of time with the final feast or banquet. So, he extends the invitation to all, through the parable, expecting a joyous response from everyone who heard it. Here we see most clearly the vision for humanity offered by God, through his son, to all people as to what life would be like when lived in communion with him. Just as with the image I offered to you at the start of this reflection of the Resurrected Lord with arms extended in welcome to all people, so here we see that the invitation offered by Jesus includes everyone. In this parable, therefore, we have what might be described as, *'The Great hope'* for humanity but what has become of it?

Surely it is the primary responsibility of the church and, in turn, all Christians to proclaim and bear witness to such good news. To make it a lived and practical reality in our own lives and in our own parishes. This invitation of Jesus surely continues to be extended today through his body on earth, the church or putting it another way the people of God.

Let us now return then to the parable itself. The first shocking thing to notice is the way in which the king's invitation to the banquet is rejected by all those who have business interests. On hearing this the king sends out a further invitation, *'Go to the street corners and invite to the banquet anyone you find.'* Such an instruction would have been outrageously shocking at the time because kings simply did not do things like that. Yet here we have reflected the very heart of Jesus and his concern for all those who are pushed to the margins of society; the poor, rejected, despised and the unloved. As a result, despite the rejected invitations God will continue to invite and the banquet will still take place. In essence, God does not change but equally he does not force either.

Imagine, if you will, what it must feel like to be invited to a banquet the like of which you have never experienced before. The servants go to the street corners and invite everyone they can find *'The good and the bad'* to come to the banquet. Now there is no hesitancy, whatsoever, in accepting the invitation because these people have nothing to lose. So, they come, because they know they have a need and that need ultimately is for God.

Once again, this parable speaks to us of the invitation sent to humanity, through his son, by God, to simply come to him. There is no force or coercion just an invitation to come to a banquet, to sit down and celebrate with each other, knowing and believing that Our Father includes everyone and excludes no one. This message is meant to be life-giving and is entrusted by Christ to his church to be proclaimed to the whole of humanity, *'come to the banquet of God where everyone is welcome, and no one is excluded.'*

Nine:

Lighting the Lamps

Matthew 25:1-13

'Am I on Fire?'

"Then the kingdom of heaven will be like this. Ten bridesmaids took their lamps and went to meet the bridegroom. Five of them were foolish, and five were wise. When the foolish took their lamps, they took no oil with them; but the wise took flasks of oil with their lamps. As the bridegroom was delayed, all of them became drowsy and slept. But at midnight there was a shout, 'Look! Here is the bridegroom! Come out to meet him.' Then all those bridesmaids[c] got up and trimmed their lamps. The foolish said to the wise, 'Give us some of your oil, for our lamps are going out.' But the wise replied, 'No! There will not be enough for you and for us; you had better go to the dealers and buy some for yourselves.' And while they went to buy it, the bridegroom came, and those who were ready went with him into the wedding banquet; and the door was shut. Later the other bridesmaids[d] came also, saying, 'Lord, lord, open to us.' But he replied, 'Truly I tell you; I do not know you.' Keep awake therefore, for you know neither the day nor the hour.

My reflection on this parable I will apply directly to myself and so will be writing in the first person, see what you think.

I find there is a need within me requiring discernment to understand what it means to be a disciple or authentic witness of Christ today. This becomes all the more important as a minister of the church because it is nothing less than a direct responsibility. Putting it simply, my vocation is to love God by loving and serving his people but putting it bluntly, am I doing it?

Perhaps this parable was written against the background of the emerging church within which there were good and bad disciples. Indeed, foolish, and wise could well be how such disciples were described. Anyway, let us see what happens. We are told that a group of women go out full of joy and excitement to meet the bridegroom, carrying their lamps. Their intention is to go with him to the wedding ceremony. However, right from the start we are told that some of them are wise whilst others are foolish.

The wise ones are different because they take with them extra oil to keep their lamps lit when their existing reservoirs run dry. The foolish ones on the other hand fail to bring the extra oil, indeed it seems that they do not even give it a second thought. Unfortunately, the bridegroom is delayed and does not arrive until midnight. At this point the wise women emerge, their lamps lit to light up to show the way. Hence, they can journey with the bridegroom all the way to the wedding hall. The foolish women, however, do not have the extra oil required at such a late hour and they have no contingency plan. Thus, when they arrive at the wedding hall the door has been closed and despite their pleas, they are told by the bridegroom, *'I tell you the truth, I don't know you.'* The parable actually ends with these challenging words, *'Therefore keep watch, because you do not know the day or the hour.'*

So, what is this parable actually saying to me? How does the parable challenge me in my ministry as a servant of Christ today? In many ways the message is obvious, but it also carries with it a sense of urgency. For me as a servant of the word who spends much of his time, reading, studying, preaching, and writing about the Gospels there is a constant need to remind myself that this alone is not enough. Rather, I need to make the Gospel a reality in the way in which I live my life. It is no use whatsoever in me becoming a so called *'expert'* in the Gospels if they do not impact on the way in which I live my life. The challenge for me, therefore, is to recognise that faith in Jesus Christ is something which must be lived. His spirit and truth must not only dwell in my heart, but it must also have a practical dimension to it. It is not enough just to know about it, but I must live it. In this way the light of Christ fuelled by my faith, must shine for others to see, by what I do as his loving servant in the world today. My studying of the scriptures may well provide some oil but that alone is not enough unless it ignites and burns for others. There can be no denying that love of God and love of neighbour is the bedrock of Jesus's teaching, but this can never be reduced to words alone. As I wait for the return of the Lord, who himself is the bridegroom, may I be like those wise women who brought with them the extra oil of faith and so lit up the way to the wedding hall.

I find myself writing these words on October 1st the memorial of Saint Therese and I conclude with what she had to say about a life of faith. In a profound and most beautiful way she describes how Jesus simply invites us to surrender to his great love. Such love is beyond our ability to comprehend for it is given overwhelmingly and unconditionally. If, however, we can see God in this way and adopt this attitude towards him and our faith, it reveals something vitally important as our starting point. That all we need to do and therefore all I need to do is surrender to his love, like a little child asleep in the arms of their father. And when I wake up, I will challenge myself with just one question, *'am I on fire with that self-same love?'*

Ten:

The Talents

Matthew 25:14-30

'Don't Bury Your Head in the Sand'

"For it is as if a man, going on a journey, summoned his slaves and entrusted his property to them; to one he gave five talents, to another two, to another one, to each according to his ability. Then he went away. The one who had received the five talents went off at once and traded with them and made five more talents. In the same way, the one who had the two talents made two more talents. But the one who had received the one talent went off and dug a hole in the ground and hid his master's money. After a long time, the master of those slaves came and settled accounts with them. Then the one who had received the five talents came forward, bringing five more talents, saying, 'Master, you handed over to me five talents; see, I have made five more talents.' His master said to him, 'Well done, good and trustworthy slave; you have been trustworthy in a few things, I will put you in charge of many things; enter into the joy of your master.' And the one with the two talents also came forward, saying, 'Master, you handed over to me two talents; see, I have made two more talents.' His master said to him, 'Well done, good and trustworthy slave; you have been trustworthy in a few things, I will put you in charge of many things; enter into the joy of your master.' Then the one who had received the one talent also came forward, saying, 'Master, I knew that you were a harsh man, reaping where you did not sow, and gathering where you did not scatter seed; so, I was afraid, and I went and hid your talent in the ground. Here you have what is yours.' But his master replied, 'You wicked and lazy slave! You knew, did you, that I reap where I did not sow, and gather where I did not scatter? Then you ought to have invested my money with the bankers, and on my return, I would have received what was my own with interest. So, take the talent from him, and give it to the one with the ten talents. For to all those who have, more will be given, and they will have an abundance; but from those who have nothing, even what they have will be taken away. As for this worthless slave, throw him into the outer darkness, where there will be weeping and gnashing of teeth.'

The thing about this parable is that it can be interpreted in so many different ways and that is kind of the point. The minute we think we know or understand everything about every parable is dangerous because we are now, in fact, failing to be open to the work of the Holy Spirit. You see it is the Holy Spirit which is ever creative moving our hearts and minds to delve deeper into the mystery of God found in the words of his son. What I offer here is one way of understanding this parable, but it is one amongst many. The important thing is for you, the reader, to spend time yourself with Christ and his word allowing the Holy Spirit to open your mind and heart to understand what this parable might mean for you and then see what happens. For this reason, I have decided to concentrate my attention, in this reflection, on the third servant for two main reasons. Firstly, his behaviour is completely different to the other two and secondly, more time in the actual text is given over to him.

The first thing to notice is the rather odd behaviour of this third servant. The previous two once given their talents set to work on multiplying what they have for their master. The third servant on the other hand simply chooses to do absolutely nothing! Well, that is not strictly speaking true, in so far as he decides to bury his talent in the ground until his master returns. When the latter arrives back, he condemns the behaviour of the third servant as being nothing less than negligent, condemning him as being lazy and irresponsible for failing to multiply his talents like the other two. So, the question remains why did the third servant act in this way and what meaning can we glean from this rather strange and, let us be honest, quite harsh parable?

Perhaps the first thing to notice is that unlike the first two servants the third does not seem to be able to relate or identify with his master. We might ask, what motivated him to behave in the way in which he did? What is lacking in this third servant which is clearly present in the other two? The answer I am suggesting is love. Therefore, we can say that this third servant did not, in fact, love his master. No, he feared him. As a result, fear became his driving force and he found strength in looking after himself. Putting it another way he sought his own security, and this became his priority. Listen to how he explained his own behaviour to his master, *'I was afraid and went out and hid your talent in the ground.'*

As a result, it would seem, that this servant failed to understand the responsibility which had been given to him. Because of his own fear he honestly believes that he is doing no less than that which his master expects, keeping the talent safe until he returns. However, he fails to grasp the need or the requirement to actually do something; that is to say to be productive with the talent which he has been given. There is, therefore, a chasm between the servant and his master through which he is unable to understand the need for him to be active and creative. This indeed is what his master expects of him, but the servant just does not see it because he has buried his head in the sand. He is like the rabbit caught in the headlights, frozen out of fear, into inactivity. We might even say he has no faith in his master because he has let fear dominate him so much to the point it has consumed him. As a result, when his master does return, he can only say, *'See, here is what belongs to you.'*

So, what does this parable mean for us and the church today? It is at this point that we need to be bold and not allow ourselves to be dominated, like the third servant, by fear. Perhaps, one of the things this parable teaches us is for the need to accept the fact that we are given responsibility, which requires us to act. It is not enough for the church or any of us who call ourselves Christian just to stand still, preserve what we have and bury our heads in the sand. No, this will not do. The Kingdom of God needs to be both proclaimed and lived, the Church is called to be a *Light to the Nations* and Jesus needs to be taught as the source of our *Hope* and *Joy*. Inevitably, this will involve both change and growth and cannot be without risk. The parable teaches us to have faith in our master, to place all our hope and trust in him, which will consequently, drive out all fear. At the same time, there is also a requirement to be active and creative in the way in which we live out our faith, looking for new ways to be the people of God in the world today. Look now at the words of the master to the servants who invested their talents, *'Come and share your master's happiness!'* Fear should never prevent us from being open to the promptings of the Holy Spirit inviting us to be alive in the world, calling us to be different, to place all our hope and trust in God and building up his Kingdom as a place where all are welcome.

Eleven:

Judged by Love

Matthew 25:31-46

'Be Merciful'

"When the Son of Man comes in his glory, and all the angels with him, then he will sit on the throne of his glory. All the nations will be gathered before him, and he will separate people one from another as a shepherd separates the sheep from the goats, and he will put the sheep at his right hand and the goats at the left. Then the king will say to those at his right hand, 'Come, you that are blessed by my Father, inherit the kingdom prepared for you from the foundation of the world; for I was hungry and you gave me food, I was thirsty and you gave me something to drink, I was a stranger and you welcomed me, I was naked and you gave me clothing, I was sick and you took care of me, I was in prison and you visited me.' Then the righteous will answer him, 'Lord, when was it that we saw you hungry and gave you food, or thirsty and gave you something to drink? And when was it that we saw you a stranger and welcomed you, or naked and gave you clothing? And when was it that we saw you sick or in prison and visited you?' And the king will answer them, 'Truly I tell you, just as you did it to one of the least of these who are members of my family, you did it to me.' Then he will say to those at his left hand, 'You that are accursed, depart from me into the eternal fire prepared for the devil and his angels; for I was hungry, and you gave me no food, I was thirsty, and you gave me nothing to drink, I was a stranger, and you did not welcome me, naked and you did not give me clothing, sick and in prison and you did not visit me.' Then they also will answer, 'Lord, when was it that we saw you hungry or thirsty or a stranger or naked or sick or in prison, and did not take care of you?' Then he will answer them, 'Truly I tell you, just as you did not do it to one of the least of these, you did not do it to me.' And these will go away into eternal punishment, but the righteous into eternal life."

Some time ago I wrote a book called, *'Sharing in the Life of God – A Journey into the Real Meaning of Easter.'* I devoted the first chapter of that book to the most fundamental question facing the human race today; *'How do we respond to suffering?'* For anyone who takes the time to read the Gospels there can be no doubt, whatsoever, that Jesus devotes much, if not most of his time, to helping people in need. Indeed, I would go as far as to say that Jesus was incapable of turning his back on anyone who was suffering in any way. In fact, I would now go even further than this by saying that Jesus not only responded to suffering but actually identified himself with it. Without doubt he reaches out to the helpless, the destitute, the despised, the unwanted, the rejected and the unloved, and responds with mercy and compassion. To those who would follow him, therefore, the essential requirement is to be like him; *'Be merciful, just as your Father is merciful.'* (Luke 6:36)

Now when we turn to this particular parable it should be no surprise at all by now to find out that the key virtue identified by Jesus is mercy or compassion. When Jesus describes the last judgement, he does so by using mercy or compassion as the keyway of identifying with him through the love and service of others. Here I am using mercy and compassion as meaning the same thing and linking both with the tenderness of God. In this parable, if you read it carefully, there is only one conclusion that any of us can come to, that Jesus identifies himself with the poor and suffering of the world.

In the parable itself all the nations of the world appear before the Son of Man, who is of course Jesus. We should note here that the term *'all'* applies to everyone with no differences between them based on colour, creed, or religion. Instead, one virtue and one alone is cited as the sole criteria for judgement and that is mercy. How have we responded to the cries of those who suffer and beg for our help?

The most important thing to note about this parable is how it is just as relevant today as it is ever was. This is the reason why I am happy to describe the Gospels as a new literary genre, which are timeless because they contain nothing less than the words of life. So, the terms of judgement are quite simple, have we responded with mercy and compassion to those who suffer, or have we chosen to walk away and turn our backs on them? Yet the parable goes deeper even than this by identifying the Son of Man with all those who suffer. As a result, to respond to those who suffer is, at the same time, to respond to the Son of Man. The text of the parable puts is like this, *'In so far as you did this to one of the least of these brothers or sisters of mine you did it to me.'* Here there is no ambiguity or confusion at all because to respond to anyone who is suffering is, at the same time, to respond to Jesus himself. Thus, by identifying with Jesus and by serving those who suffer results in nothing less than communion with God himself, the road to which ultimately leads to the Kingdom. Such acts of mercy, compassion, forgiveness, and love finds the Son of Man saying, *'Come, you that are blessed by my Father, inherit the kingdom prepared for you since the foundation of the world.'*

However, there are also words for those who have not acted with mercy or compassion towards the suffering of the world and in so doing have not identified themselves or their actions with Jesus, *'In so far as you neglected to do this to one of the least of these, you neglected to do it to me.'* These are those people who simply turned their backs on suffering humanity and walked away not only from them but also from Christ himself. As a result, such people are now told simply to, *'Go away.'*

So, what does this all mean for those who would follow Christ now? The answer to this question is, in fact, quite simple and yet challenging because it is a call to action. The challenge of our Christian lives and whether or not we walk in the footsteps of Jesus rests upon our response to suffering humanity. Just as Jesus never turned his back on anyone in need, so we too must find him, serve him, and love him in all those we come across who suffer. That according to Jesus, himself, is the sole criteria of judgement but it requires a response not at some distant time in the future but here and now. To finish, Saint John of the Cross put it like this, *'At the evening of life, we shall be judged on our love.'* Jesus in this parable tells us clearly what this actually means.

Twelve:

Salt and Light

Matthew 5:13-16

'You'

"You are the salt of the earth; but if salt has lost its taste, how can its saltiness be restored? It is no longer good for anything but is thrown out and trampled underfoot.

"You are the light of the world. A city built on a hill cannot be hid. No one after lighting a lamp puts it under the bushel basket, but on the lampstand, and it gives light to all in the house. In the same way, let your light shine before others, so that they may see your good works and give glory to your Father in heaven.

'You are the salt of the earth.'

'You are the light of the world.'

We need to read this parable in such a way that it impacts directly on our lives today, hence my emphasis on the word, *'You,'* in my introduction. Yet before we do so I want to suggest that we all have a problem, and it is this that most of us do not know who we really are. Several years ago, I spent some time reflecting on the genealogy of Jesus Christ in Matthew's Gospel. (Matthew 1:1-16) In the end, I came to a remarkable conclusion. You see it is possible to divide the genealogy into three main groups. The first includes the Patriarchs, the second the Kings and the third are a group of people we know virtually nothing about. For this reason, I described them as, *'nothings and nobodies.'* Yet it is this group of the *unknowns* of the world, which eventually led to the birth of Jesus. What then does this say about the importance of status and power?

Many of us crave importance and demand recognition of some kind. We want positions of responsibility and need others to look up to and respect us. Yet how far is this from the Gospel of Jesus Christ? When the disciples were arguing amongst themselves as to who was the greatest amongst them, Jesus responded by saying,

'If anyone wants to be first, he must make himself last of all and servant of all.' (Mark 9:30-37) When the disciples tried to stop children from getting close to Jesus he said, *'Let the little children come to me; for it is to such as these that the kingdom of God belongs.'* (Mark 10:13-16) What then can we learn from all of this?

Many of us fall into the trap of believing in our own sense of self-importance and spend much time attempting to justify it. It can even be worse than this when we turn to criticising others because of their failures to live up to our expectations when it comes to practicing their faith. How are we then witnesses to the Gospel of Jesus Christ? Perhaps this is what Jesus means when he talks about *'Salt losing its saltiness'* and *'putting a lamp under a bowl.'*

So, what then are we called to be and do? How can we be *'salt'* and *'light'* for the world? Well, first and foremost all we have to be is ourselves, *'nothings and nobodies,'* because such people are fine to God. We need to be comfortable with who we are and believe with God that will always be enough. This is because above and beyond everything else we are invited by Jesus to be witnesses to the Gospel and this is something that we cannot do if we are obsessed with ourselves. It is important that we recognise this trait and resist giving into it because it leads to hypocrisy. Putting it simply I do not need power, qualifications, or a position of responsibility to love God or indeed to be loved by him. Instead, I need to offer the world what Jesus offers me, his love. Hence, the key to everything is to understand that although in the eyes of the world I might well be classified as a *'nothing and a nobody'* to God I am loved beyond anything I could ever imagine and that is what really matters.

Jesus actually warns us that *'salt'* can become *'tasteless'* and we have to have the courage and the maturity to challenge ourselves by asking, *'am I really an authentic witness to the selfless love of God as revealed in his son Jesus Christ?'*

'Neither do people light a lamp and put it under a bowl.' In these words, Jesus is really inviting us to be the light of his love in the world, for others. Putting it simply, we are called to live good lives, to be a holy people, and reflect something of the nature of God's

compassion for everyone. Ultimately Jesus only gave one commandment to his disciples and in turn us, *'Love one another, just as I have loved you. By this everyone will know that you are my disciples if you have love for one another.'* (John 13:34-35)

The simple truth is that God's love cannot be earned, rather it is given as a free gift. So, we need to stop all that activity and recognise that no good can, in fact, be done except through the power of God. In other words, Jesus wants us to understand that God's goodness flows out of us simply by recognising that he loves us just as we are. If we are to achieve this, however, we need to spend time with God, just letting him love us and so appreciating that he is the source of our strength and any good that we might do. By living simple lives of love and service Jesus's light shines through, so that we become living flames of his love.

In his book *'Let Us Dream,'* Pope Francis puts it like this, *'Our greatest power is not in the respect that others have for us, but in the service, we can offer others.'* (Simon and Schuster 2020, page 127)

Thirteen:

Sand or Rock?

Matthew 7:21-27

'Be warned!'

"Not everyone who says to me, 'Lord, Lord,' will enter the kingdom of heaven, but only the one who does the will of my Father in heaven. On that day many will say to me, 'Lord, Lord, did we not prophesy in your name, and cast out demons in your name, and do many deeds of power in your name?' Then I will declare to them, 'I never knew you; go away from me, you evildoers.'

"Everyone then who hears these words of mine and acts on them will be like a wise man who built his house on rock. The rain fell, the floods came, and the winds blew and beat on that house, but it did not fall, because it had been founded on rock. And everyone who hears these words of mine and does not act on them will be like a foolish man who built his house on sand. The rain fell, and the floods came, and the winds blew and beat against that house, and it fell—and great was its fall!"

This is one of those parables which emphasises the importance of action. The premise is a simple one, a wise person gives careful thought and planning to the building of their house. As a result, the most important thing to do is to make sure that the house is built on a firm foundation, which here means rock. The foolish person, however, does not do this. Rather they build their house on sand. Thus, when the wind, rain and storms come, the house built on rock remains standing, whilst the one built on sand collapses. We now must ask ourselves, what does this mean and how does it affect our lives of faith today.

Perhaps the first point to make is about the actual words of Jesus. There can be little doubt that in the days of the early church such words were given a high degree of importance. The point has already been made earlier in this project that, in my opinion, the words of Jesus are so radically different that they deserve to be classified as a new literary genre. To the early Christians and indeed to us today they are the timeless words of life. Indeed, in Matthew's Gospel we have Jesus himself saying, *'Heaven and earth will pass away, but my words will never pass away.'* Now the words of Jesus gave meaning to their lives, filling their hearts with his resurrected presence. With his peace and joy consuming their whole lives they were now able to see themselves and the world differently, but they were also acutely aware of something else, that those same words of life were also a call to action.

This now leads us to making a remarkable claim, that to be a follower of Jesus must involve doing something. Or putting it another way, it is not enough just to read or hear the words, they must be lived. It is, therefore, the responsibility of Christians to make the Gospel of Jesus Christ a living reality in our lives today by putting them into practice. If we refuse or fail to do this then we run the risk of leaving Jesus's words on a page in a book and quite rightly this makes us look foolish because we are.

When those early Christians heard this parable for the first time, they came to one simple conclusion, that they must be put into practice. They must have an impact on their lives to the point that others would look at them and say, *'why are they living their lives so differently to everybody else?'* In this way the foundations of the church would be built on the rock of Jesus's words, which would ultimately lead to a better world for all people.

Now let us come back to the world of today, the church and the way in which we live our lives of faith. At this point we need to be honest and brave by admitting the fact that this parable contains a serious warning. To this end, it provides us with a startling choice whether to build the church and our faith on the rock of Jesus Christ or whether to build on sand which, in reality, has nothing to do with the Gospel at all.

What then is required you might ask? Perhaps the best way is to go back to the days of the early church and reflect on what they did. We have already made the point that their lives were transformed by the words of the risen Christ. Those early brothers and sisters saw the Gospel in its simplicity and made the choice to live it and it changed their lives for ever, *By this (love) everyone will know that you are my disciples, if you love one another.* (John 13:35) Ask yourself this question then, when people look at the church today, what do they see? Are they inspired by an organisation dedicated and committed to the poor, unwanted, despised and rejected? Do they see an institution not motivated by power, control, wealth, and manipulation but one inspired by service and love with mercy and compassion at its heart? Do they see people motivated to put into action the words of Jesus found in his parables, which reveal not only the nature of God but what it actually means to follow him? Do they see a Church called by Christ himself to be a *light to the nations* and point to him as the source of our *hope and joy*? If they do then this is the Church built on rock but if they do not, then perhaps they see nothing, because such a church has been washed away as its foundation was only built sand.

Part Two:

Mark

'He did not speak to them except in parables,
but he explained everything in private to his disciples.'
(Mark 4:34)

One:

The Seed So Small

Mark 4:26-34

'What can I do?'

He also said, "The kingdom of God is as if someone would scatter seed on the ground, and would sleep and rise night and day, and the seed would sprout and grow, he does not know how. The earth produces of itself, first the stalk, then the head, then the full grain in the head. But when the grain is ripe, at once he goes in with his sickle, because the harvest has come."

He also said, "With what can we compare the kingdom of God, or what parable will we use for it? It is like a mustard seed, which, when sown upon the ground, is the smallest of all the seeds on earth; yet when it is sown it grows up and becomes the greatest of all shrubs, and puts forth large branches, so that the birds of the air can make nests in its shade."

With many such parables he spoke the word to them, as they were able to hear it; he did not speak to them except in parables, but he explained everything in private to his disciples

I remember once being in a classroom discussing this parable with a group of children. We came to the conclusion that the parable is telling us that the Kingdom of God grows slowly, out of sight, unseen and often without us knowing about it. The mustard seed is one of the smallest seeds of all, yet in the end it grows into one of the biggest shrubs, so big that the birds of the air come and perch in its branches. We then went on to discuss what this parable means for us and our lives of faith today. Ultimately, we found ourselves reflecting on the state of the world; wars, famine and starvation, poverty, refugees and the suffering and pain of humanity all of us see, every day, on the news.

'So how does the parable fit into all of that then?' one of the children asked? My response was to ask them, *'whom do you think Jesus is talking to when he told this story?'* One of the children immediately

said, '*Us!*'

'*But we're only little kids,*' one of his classmates replied back.

'*Yes, like the seeds, they were little, just like us!*' was his friend's sharp response.

At this point I wanted the children, themselves, to delve deeper into what they believed Jesus was saying to them. So, I continued, '*What do you think Jesus might be asking you to do about the world then and all those people who are suffering?*'

'*Don't know but I think he's asking us to do something,*' was the initial response.

'*We could collect money for charity and send it to people who need it,*' another child said.

'*Yes, but we've got no money,*' his friend replied.

At this point one little girl put her hand in her pocket, pulled out a coin and held it in the air before saying, '*I've got a penny!*'

Of course, as you might expect, this was greeted with howls of laughter by the rest of her classmates. When things, eventually, calmed down the boy next to her remarked, '*One penny's not going to help many people is it?*'

But the girl with tears in her eyes was persistent, '*No,*' she *said, 'but if we collected one penny from everybody living in this country that would be a lot of pennies and a lot of money wouldn't it?*'

At this point the whole class, along with myself, were, literally, stunned into silence because the little girl was right. All of a sudden, I realised that this is exactly what Jesus was teaching in so many different ways through this parable. It is the little things, which ultimately matter. Here we had a little girl listening to the words of Jesus and something awakened within her heart of faith. The seed began to grow and touched our hearts too. Small things do matter and in that little girl I recognised the potential for humanity God sees in each and every single one of us. I found the whole experience extremely humbling and yet here it was, grace in action, right before our very eyes. This is what the

Kingdom of God is like, the seed growing quietly, slowly, unnoticed, and yet revealing what we are truly capable of.

When I walked into the classroom that day, hand on heart, I never expected to experience God like that. I went in thinking that, somehow, I was bringing God to them, when, in fact, it was the children who revealed the true nature and being of God to me. In that child I recognised something which Jesus wants all of us to see and that is the potential to grow. No matter how bad the world appears to be, no matter how overwhelming the odds are, no matter how much suffering we are surrounded by, we all have the capacity and the ability to respond.

On that day I grasped something that Jesus, in the parable, was drawing our attention to and that is to appreciate the little things. We do not have to be significant, in the eyes of the world, to be part of God's plan for salvation. Small gestures, little actions are all seeds of the Kingdom of God, which any of us can reveal in our lives of faith. The world might well be a dark and sad place, but it can be lit up by the smallest acts of kindness.

I left the classroom that day with a smile on my face, a spring in my step and the recognition that the seed of faith was alive and kicking in my heart too. The next thing for me to do now was something small to bring light into the life of someone else. Now what about you?

Two:

New Wine into Fresh Skins

Mark 2:18-22

'Something new is here'

Now John's disciples and the Pharisees were fasting; and people came and said to him, "Why do John's disciples and the disciples of the Pharisees fast, but your disciples do not fast?" Jesus said to them, "The wedding guests cannot fast while the bridegroom is with them, can they? As long as they have the bridegroom with them, they cannot fast. The days will come when the bridegroom is taken away from them, and then they will fast on that day.

"No one sews a piece of unshrunk cloth on an old cloak; otherwise, the patch pulls away from it, the new from the old, and a worse tear is made. And no one puts new wine into old wineskins; otherwise, the wine will burst the skins, and the wine is lost, and so are the skins; but one puts new wine into fresh wineskins."

I have met many Christians in my life who seem to only know the God who might best be described as the God of anger. Here God is perceived as a judge who constantly updates and records all the mistakes, we make in life so that one day he will punish us for our transgressions. Such an image of God portrays him as vindictive and severe requiring those who believe in him to do whatever they can to pacify his discontent. This, however, is something no one can escape from and so the only thing to do is follow a prescribed set of rules, which might, one day, somehow deflect some of that anger. People who live their lives carrying an image of God like that around with them are often wracked with guilt because no matter what they do or how hard they try nothing ever seems good enough for a God like that. In such situation's faith is not life giving, faith does not set people free, instead it stifles and suffocates them. To be honest, I find this incredibly sad because it bears no resemblance at all to the Father revealed by Jesus Christ. The source of this has to be bad teaching and poor formation in the faith, there is no other reasonable explanation because the people I am talking about here are, more often than not, regular church goers.

This is why this short parable told by Jesus is so important. When Jesus says, *'No! New wine into fresh skins!'* he is telling us that something new is here. This of course is, in fact, Jesus himself. You see Jesus comes to reveal in his own life what God is really like. For him the Father is not consumed with anger and frustration, who will return one day to punish all those who have failed to follow a prescribed set of rules. If people, in fact, perceive God in this way, Jesus in the parable is, in effect, saying, *'No!'* Instead, he reveals his Father as the God of mercy, compassion, forgiveness, and love. Indeed, such a Father loves all people, including sinners, in exactly the same way. Here when I say all people that is exactly what I mean, the whole of humanity, leaving nobody out. Such a God desires only what is good for us and therefore never seeks to harm us.

Let us now see how this works in action but the only way to do this is by reference to the life of Jesus himself because in his life we see what the Farther is really like. Think about it, with whom does Jesus spend much of his time? The answer is, of course, with sinners. Then think about, what does Jesus actually do? He heals the sick, welcomes those who are rejected, despised, unwanted and unloved. He forgives transgressions, frees people from evil, seeks out the lost and assures everyone of God's love. Compare this with the religious leaders of the day like the Pharisees who taught that only by following the letter of the Law could people be saved. Yet in Jesus, something new had arrived.

Jesus does not threaten or frighten people with the anger of a punishing God, instead the reverse is true. He wants people to relate to their Father in a completely different way. For Jesus God only desires what is good for us. He wants us to approach our Father by seeing him as welcoming with arms open wide. This God wants us to be free, to be happy and to live in peace with each other and with him. Ultimately Jesus wants us to believe that Our Father loves us more than we could ever know and all we have to do in return is love him and love each other in the same way. As a result, God becomes the source of our freedom, he loves us unconditionally, is merciful and tender-hearted. He is the source of our life, of our joy and of all our hopes. He wants us to live life to the full and be happy by resting in him. In revealing all of this Jesus was saying, something new is here.

So, to all those people who have an unhealthy image of or relationship with God I would say, look to the Father revealed by Jesus and find, perhaps for the first time in your life, something completely different. This is the God of unconditional love, who loves us no matter what and in whom we all can be healed. Of course, not all those who heard this message believed or accepted it and, if truth be told, we are still to this day struggling to come to terms with it. But it is there on every page of the Gospels inviting us to come to the Father, through Jesus, where we will, in fact, find both our true selves and our real home. Yet we have to be brave because it can involve a complete transformation in the way we relate to and understand God. This is not something new because this is exactly what Jesus was saying when he said, *'No! New wine into fresh skins.'*

Three:

Be on Guard

Mark 13: 33-37

'Wake-up and watch'

"Beware, keep alert; for you do not know when the time will come. It is like a man going on a journey, when he leaves home and puts his slaves in charge, each with his work, and commands the doorkeeper to be on the watch. Therefore, keep awake—for you do not know when the master of the house will come, in the evening, or at midnight, or at cockcrow, or at dawn, or else he may find you asleep when he comes suddenly. And what I say to you I say to all: Keep awake."

How would you describe your faith and your relationship with Jesus? Is it alive and exciting? Are you motivated by the Gospel? If asked would you say you are deeply in love with Christ? Are you enthused by the mission given to you by God to the point that you are excited because your life has a meaning and that you are part of his plan for the salvation of the world?

We normally find this parable read on the first Sunday of Advent and it serves as a wake-up call to our faith. Look at the opening sentences, *'Be on guard! Be alert!'* Later we are told to, *'Keep watch,'* and finally to, *'Stay awake'* so, something is going on here, the only question is, what? The early Christians had no doubt that Jesus would keep his promise and return within their own lifetimes. As a result, their primary desire was to be, literally, with Christ as soon as possible. So, they waited and prepared for the coming of the Lord with heart-felt enthusiasm, after all it could be any day or any minute. However, as time went by, they were presented with a problem when Jesus did not return. What happens when their enthusiasm for him, his teaching and his Gospel begins to wane?

As a result, the early Christian communities began, in earnest, to concern themselves with keeping their memories and relationship with the Lord alive. They could not afford for their enthusiasm for him and the Gospel to diminish. Perhaps some thought they would forget him or that as time went by, they would compromise his teaching and therefore fall short of what the Gospel demanded. Equally there was the problem of apathy or that faith was becoming little more than a routine. Does this sound familiar because we face the same kind of issues today; do we not?

The way those early Christians guarded against such concerns was to emphasise what we find in this parable and as a result certain phrases and words were emphasised and repeated over and over again, *'Watch, remain alert, stay awake.'* Yet the interesting thing we actually discover in this parable is that Jesus meant these words not just for those who heard them for the first time but also for us today when he says, *'What I say to you, I say to everyone: watch!'* In this way the words of Christ are addressed to all Christians for all time.

So, here we find ourselves two millennia later, are we awake and alert? Are we keeping watch? Or are we now suffering from what those early Christians feared so much apathy, compromise, and indifference towards the Gospel. Has the memory of Jesus faded in our minds? Have we drifted into routine? Are our hearts on fire with love for him in the sure and certain knowledge that he loved us first? Do we have the courage to even ask these questions? Do we even want to ask them?

What do we need to do then? Well in the first instance Jesus tells us, *'Be on guard! Be alert.'* But to do this we must go back to Christ himself. This means we must recognise that only he can awaken something within us that no one and nothing else can. So, first and foremost and above all things we need to learn how to fall in love with Jesus. We need to recognise how he attracts us and seduces us through his overwhelming and unconditional love to the point that all we want to do in return is, to know, love and serve him. Perhaps the starting point to all of this is to recognise that we are asleep in the first place and not just us but perhaps, dare I say it, the church too.

When others look at us what do they see? Do they see apathy and indifference because we are asleep when it comes to the radical love taught and lived by Jesus Christ? Perhaps we need to take a good hard look at ourselves and ask such difficult questions? Or do they see something else, a church alive with the presence of Christ, constantly mediating his love. Because if all people do see is a sleeping institution going through the motions, who will be attracted by that? What future does such a church have and here we find ourselves sharing the same concerns of our brothers and sisters all those centuries ago. The difference is, of course, that they did something about it and so must we.

So, we must go back to our source because only Christ can waken us from such slumber. We need first and foremost to deepen our relationship with him because only he can fill us with the grace, we need to love others in the same way he loves us. Our hearts and lives need to be full of the hope and joy, which only faith in him can provide. We need to really believe that through us living such lives others will experience Jesus and when that happens people will be both attracted to him and their lives transformed. Surely this is the primary mission of the church. A mission given to it by Christ himself and to be offered to all people.

Hence it is time to, *'Be on guard and to be alert!'*

Four:

When Jesus Returns

Mark 13:24-32

'Everything will change'

"But in those days, after that suffering, the sun will be darkened, and the moon will not give its light, and the stars will be falling from heaven, and the powers in the heavens will be shaken.

Then they will see 'the Son of Man coming in clouds' with great power and glory. Then he will send out the angels, and gather his elect from the four winds, from the ends of the earth to the ends of heaven.

"From the fig tree learn its lesson: as soon as its branch becomes tender and puts forth its leaves, you know that summer is near. So also, when you see these things taking place, you know that he is near, at the very gates. Truly I tell you, this generation will not pass away until all these things have taken place. Heaven and earth will pass away, but my words will not pass away.

"But about that day or hour no one knows, neither the angels in heaven, nor the Son, but only the Father.

To understand the parable of the fig tree we need to place it within the context of the whole passage which focuses on what is of often called the end times. I can remember some time ago looking at the Sunday Gospel readings for the thirty-third week in ordinary time and thinking to myself, '*I am a little relieved not be preaching that week.*' Then the Holy Spirit took over. When I should have been preaching, I fell ill and the next available slot was, you guessed it, the thirty-third Sunday in ordinary time, with the theme of the end of the world. At the same time, I was asked to write something for the parish newsletter as I was preaching that week. Then when one of the parishioner's learnt it was going to be me at the lectern next weekend he said, '*Tell them the end is nigh!*' Finally, another member of the parish shared with me the reason why his son had stopped going to church, '*It had become too soft,*' he said.

If truth be told, I felt a bit like the prophet Jonah who desperately tried to avoid God but found him wherever he went. So, in the end, I just had to give in and co-operate with what God was obviously inviting me to do. The passage starts with a description of what sounds like the end of the world. If we take this literally scientists tell us that one day the sun will burn itself out, the moon will drift away into space and the stars will literally collapse, all of which means there can be no life on earth. On the other hand, theologians tell us that the words are meant to be interpreted symbolically, just as Jesus used the ordinary things of everyday life like seeds, bread, wine, sheep, shepherds and so on and infused them with meaning, so he does the same here with the sun, moon, and stars. When we link this to the parable of the fig tree a meaning emerges, which is that things will not remain as they are for ever. When we look at the world around us, we see war, terrorism, global warming, disasters, poverty, and injustice. At the sight of such things some of us are, at least at times, tempted to be negative and out of sheer frustration with the status quo cry out, *'The end is nigh!'* Yet is this what Jesus is telling us to do?

The Gospel is meant to fill our hearts with *hope* and *joy*, and therefore we need to read the rest of the passage before coming to any conclusions. The first thing to note, is how we are told Jesus will keep his promise and return and when he does everything will change and the world will never be the same again. At this point there is no hint, in Mark, of condemnation, judgment or punishment. Instead, the Lord gathers the people to himself, *'From the ends of the earth to the ends of the heavens.'* What a beautiful image this is of Jesus gathering his people around him.

The Eucharist, Holy Communion or the Mass is a foretaste of this great event. Here the Lord stands in the middle of his gathered people and shares his very life with them pouring out his love on everyone and exhorting them to do the same for each other in return. One day when he returns everything will change but until then we are given a foretaste of what life will be like when that happens.

But what are we to do until this great event takes place? Jesus goes on to tell us, *'Heaven and earth will pass away, but my words will never pass away.'* Therefore, we need to cling to them and live them with every fibre of our being. Summarising the teaching of Jesus in the Gospel of Mark we are now able to say, when the world refuses to show mercy, we must always be merciful. When the world refuses to forgive we must always forgive and when the world refuses to love we must always love one another in the same way he loves us. Now you do not need me to tell you just how hard this teaching is to put into practice, but I will ask a question myself, when the church does this has it gone soft or is it simply bearing witness to the Gospel of Jesus Christ?

Jesus is telling us here that his words have the power to save but they must be both cherished and lived. Hence part of the vocation of all those who would follow Christ and call themselves Christian is to give others a foretaste of what life will be like when he returns. Jesus comes to bring about the salvation of the world and needs not the light of the sun because he is the source of all light. Hence when he comes all injustice will cease, famine, poverty, oppression, corruption, and persecution will come to an end. Yet he does not threaten but brings only the peace that he can give. Our role now, at least in part, is to give others a foretaste of what this will be like. We do this by reaching out to the poor and the marginalised and doing whatever we can to help them. We do this by being kind, gentle and tender-hearted. We do this by being instruments of his mercy, compassion, forgiveness, and love. We do this by letting others know that they are not alone in the darkness and that there is always someone there willing to hold their hand. We do this by speaking up for those who cannot speak for themselves, the homeless and the destitute, the refugee and the asylum seeker. We do this by giving people the time and the care they need when no one else will. We do this by being people of hope, by being positive and by living lives which give expression to the words of Christ, which will never pass away. We do this by knowing and believing that we are already embraced by Jesus. We do this because this is what Christ has asked us to do in his name.

One day everything will come to an end and everything will change but until then, we love, and we go on loving until that day when we are consumed by the source of love itself.

Five:

Letting Go to Find God

Mark 7:1-8 and 14-23

'What matters most?'

Now when the Pharisees and some of the scribes who had come from Jerusalem gathered around him, they noticed that some of his disciples were eating with defiled hands, that is, without washing them. (For the Pharisees, and all the Jews, do not eat unless they thoroughly wash their hands, thus observing the tradition of the elders; and they do not eat anything from the market unless they wash it; and there are also many other traditions that they observe, the washing of cups, pots, and bronze kettles.) So the Pharisees and the scribes asked him, "Why do your disciples not live according to the tradition of the elders, but eat with defiled hands?" He said to them, "Isaiah prophesied rightly about you hypocrites, as it is written, 'This people honours me with their lips, but their hearts are far from me in vain do they worship me, teaching human precepts as doctrines.'

You abandon the commandment of God and hold to human tradition."

Then he called the crowd again and said to them, "Listen to me, all of you, and understand: there is nothing outside a person that by going in can defile, but the things that come out are what defile."

When he had left the crowd and entered the house, his disciples asked him about the parable. He said to them, "Then do you also fail to understand? Do you not see that whatever goes into a person from outside cannot defile, since it enters, not the heart but the stomach, and goes out into the sewer?" (Thus he declared all foods clean.) And he said, "It is what comes out of a person that defiles. For it is from within, from the human heart, that evil intentions come: fornication, theft, murder, adultery, avarice, wickedness, deceit, licentiousness, envy, slander, pride, folly. All these evil things come from within, and they defile a person."

If you were asked to describe Jesus in one word, what would it be? I would have to use the word *love* in its fullest sense and this parable encourages us to do the same. Yet it also challenges us to make a choice between Jesus on the one hand and human traditions on the other. As we read this parable and the surrounding text, what emerges is the source of Jesus's conflict with the religious leaders of the day. There can be no doubt that Jesus confronts them with something new in terms of what it means to be faithful to God. In response they are constrained by their blind observance of the Law which prevents them from understanding what Jesus is really saying. In essence Jesus offers the God of *love* whilst the religious teachers cannot see beyond the need to be faithful and, therefore, obedient to the Law.

It comes as no surprise then that the Pharisees are far from happy when they see the disciples of Jesus eating with unclean hands. Hence, they challenge him by asking, *'Why do your disciples not follow the traditions of the elders?'* In reading this, it is possible to see that their animosity is aimed directly at Jesus himself through the behaviour of his disciples. Interestingly, however, the Pharisees are, in fact, right because Jesus is seeking to break the bond of blind obedience to tradition and replace it with something else, *love.*

There is something absent from the hearts of the religious leaders who consistently attack Jesus and are both unable and unwilling to understand what he is really saying about the Kingdom of God and that again is, *love.* For them the Law of God is so bound to human tradition that they cannot see the difference between the two. Hence what they teach is a set of rules and regulations established by the elders which must be followed slavishly by the people if God's will is to be done. What is absent from this is *love* and the good of the people entrusted to their care. For them nothing is more important than living lives which conform exactly to their teaching whether the people can follow them or not. In fact, it gets worse because the conclusion they come to is shocking. If you cannot follow the Law and all its associated traditions, then you cannot be faithful to God and if you cannot be faithful to God then he rejects you.

We can now begin to understand why Jesus responds to such teaching with harsh words of his own, *'You let go of the commands of*

God and are holding on to the traditions of men.' The mistake the Pharisees make is to equate the traditions of the elders with the will of God so that the two, in effect, become the same thing. Jesus on the other hands appears to be pointing this serious error out by making it clear that the two are not the same because one of them has nothing to do with the will of his Father.

Now let us jump forward to the present day and be brave enough to place ourselves in the same situation. So, the first thing we need to ask ourselves is that in following Jesus what matters the most? The answer must be, of course, *love*. Yet we can still fall into the same trap as the Pharisees by elevating the importance of human tradition. As a result, the church and all of us who call ourselves Christian must distinguish between being faithful to Christ and preserving human traditions, which can stifle our *love* for him and each other. This is not an easy task, but we can link it to what people and the world actually need. Think of it like this, are people attracted to a church with Christ as its beating heart, pouring out his overwhelming love for all people, or in an institution obsessed with preserving human traditions? Does being faithful to the Gospel involve *loving* God and *loving* our neighbour or being blindly obedient to a set of rules and regulations which owe their origin to our ancestors? The former means that God lives in and through his church and his people, whilst the latter means we are merely repeating the past. The great sadness here is that we end up burying Christ in the tomb again, our great treasure of such great value becomes lost, and his gentle face obscured to the point that no one can even recognise him anymore.

Sacred tradition needs to be valued but not confused with that created by people. Its role is to bring us closer to Christ and each other not drive us away. Jesus makes it very clear in his confrontation with the religious leaders of the day that the overwhelming law of God is *love*. Nothing can contradict this, and everything must point towards it. Ultimately Jesus gave us one commandment, to *love* one another, in the same way he *loves* us; if we can find it in our hearts to *love* like that, above all things, then the Kingdom of Heaven will always be nearer to us than we could ever imagine.

Six:

The Spirit Within

Mark 3:20-35

'United we stand but divided we fall'

And the crowd came together again, so that they could not even eat. When his family heard it, they went out to restrain him, for people were saying, "He has gone out of his mind." And the scribes who came down from Jerusalem said, "He has Beelzebub, and by the ruler of the demons he casts out demons." And he called them to him, and spoke to them in parables, "How can Satan cast out Satan? If a kingdom is divided against itself, that kingdom cannot stand. And if a house is divided against itself, that house will not be able to stand. And if Satan has risen up against himself and is divided, he cannot stand, but his end has come. But no one can enter a strong man's house and plunder his property without first tying up the strong man; then indeed the house can be plundered.

"Truly I tell you, people will be forgiven for their sins and whatever blasphemies they utter; but whoever blasphemes against the Holy Spirit can never have forgiveness, but is guilty of an eternal sin"— for they had said, "He has an unclean spirit."

Then his mother and his brothers came; and standing outside, they sent to him and called him. A crowd was sitting around him; and they said to him, "Your mother and your brothers and sisters are outside, asking for you." And he replied, "Who are my mother and my brothers?" And looking at those who sat around him, he said, "Here are my mother and my brothers! Whoever does the will of God is my brother and sister and mother."

Have you ever felt divided within or not at ease with yourself? Have you ever felt that there was something not quite right about your life, that there was, in fact, something missing but you did not know what? Have you ever asked deep questions about the meaning of life or existence, such as, why are we here and what is life for? To attempt to answer questions such as these involves taking the time to make what is known as the journey within. This is a search to penetrate the mystery of life, which in the end only God can answer. If we do not do this then we can end up living our lives on the surface, struggling to come to terms with who we really are, which can, in turn, give rise to serious mental health issues. After all, *'why am I here and what does life mean?'*

The suggestion being made here is that the mystery of God and therefore of the Holy Spirit lies deep within our own hearts just waiting to be discovered. Yet, the search for meaning within takes time, energy, and effort. In his book *'Confessions'* Saint Augustine once said, *'Our hearts are restless, until they rest in you.'* Such restlessness, for some people, can often be seen as problematical, whilst for others it is nothing less than the stirrings of the Holy Spirit inviting us to make the journey within. The Spirit is, of course, there to help us and guide us to the Father who just, as with the *'Lost Son,'* simply waits for us to come home.

Responding to such restlessness can result in co-operating with the Holy Spirit in our quest to find meaning, purpose, and value in life. At the same time, it can also be part of a process involving, perhaps for the first time in our lives, the journey within, one which eventually will lead us home and to union with the Father. When this happens, we will receive a strength which not even Satan himself can break. Discovering the truth that the Holy Spirit dwells within our own hearts' changes everything. Suddenly, there is a reason to live, and life has a purpose. We find and experience a joy we thought never existed and become energised as a result. Then we experience a love beyond all understanding and our relationship with ourselves, other people and God is transformed. Now the world is a different place because the Holy Spirit has set us free.

This is true for all people and lies waiting to be discovered in the depths of all our hearts. Yet God never forces us but rather simply invites us to co-operate with him. It is like discovering a tiny spark within and fanning it with the little faith we have until it becomes a raging fire. When that happens, everything changes, and nothing will ever be the same again. What potential we all have to realise our true humanity and therefore to become ever more like Christ. On that day we become like the strong man who will not let anyone break into his house and steal his possessions because we have the Holy Spirit who is the origin and source of all our strength, in him we place all our trust, and he will not fail us. This short parable is an exhortation to rely on God rather than on ourselves. It invites us to recognise that there is something beyond us, the Holy Spirit, who will, if we let him, transform our lives forever. This life-giving Spirit of grace may appear, at first, to be nothing more than a shadow almost beyond our grasp and yet it is the source, ultimately, of the strong man's strength. We are invited to build our lives, through faith, on such grace and when we do, on that day, we will realise, perhaps for the first time in our lives that nothing can separate us from the love of God revealed in Christ Jesus, Our Lord.

Seven:

The Lamp and the Light

Mark 4: 21-25

'What must I do?'

He said to them, "Is a lamp brought in to be put under the bushel basket, or under the bed, and not on the lampstand? For there is nothing hidden, except to be disclosed; nor is anything secret, except to come to light. Let anyone with ears to hear listen!" And he said to them, "Pay attention to what you hear; the measure you give will be the measure you get, and still more will be given you. For to those who have, more will be given; and from those who have nothing, even what they have will be taken away."

For this reflection I am going to begin with a rather bold statement, which is that most people these days do not read the Bible. Assuming this is true then again, most people, will get their impression of what God is like from those who both read the Bible and practice the faith of Christianity. In other words, they read us. This brings with it a huge responsibility and the parable of the Lamp is used by Jesus to make this exact same point.

The interesting thing about Mark chapter four is that it begins with the parable of the Sower one which we have covered elsewhere in this book. However, it is important to note that there is a direct connection between the two parables. For a start Jesus explains the meaning of the parable of the Sower to his disciples, a practice which he rarely observes, *'To you is granted the secret of the kingdom, but to those who are outside everything comes in parables.'* Eventually Jesus makes the point that the Sower is all about listening to, understanding, and implementing his word. In other words, it is about living a life of faith as an expression of placing all our trust in God.

The parable of the Lamp comes directly after Jesus takes his disciples to one side and, as we have seen, shares the meaning of the Sower with them. Now he takes a humble clay lamp with a small reservoir of oil at one end and a wick fed through its neck at the other, which would have been placed on a shelf in a room to maximise the light it shed, to further illustrate what believing in him actually means. Once again, Jesus makes the point, *'For there is nothing hidden except to be disclosed, nothing kept secret except to be brought to light.'* Christianity is not some secret cult or sect but a faith to be lived, professed, and borne witness to, hence the light shining for all to see. Those who grasp this are like the disciples and the good seed in which the word of God grew to yield a rich harvest. Yet such faith is not to be kept to ourselves, rather it must be lived and shared. It must shine like the lamp in the darkness for all to see.

Biblical scholars often make the point that the Gospel of Mark was probably written in Rome when Christianity was facing great persecution under the emperor Nero. The parable of the Lamp urges followers of Jesus to bear witness to their faith even though they faced the possibility of torture and even death. However, we still need to understand what this means and how it affects us today. For those early Christians to proclaim Jesus as the Son of God was effectively to deny the divinity of the emperor and hence its proponents were classified as not only being disloyal to him but of treason to Rome itself. There are, in fact, many Christians in various parts of the world today who are being persecuted for their faith and as a result facing, imprisonment, denial of their human rights, torture, discrimination and even death. Thankfully, however, most Christians in the western world, at least, are not facing such atrocities. Yet there are specific ways that Christianity, even here, is under attack and by this I am talking about secularism and materialism both of which, whether intentionally or not, seek to undermine the values upon which the faith is based. What then under such circumstances is the follower of Christ expected to do?

Here we need to go back to the parable itself. Jesus tells us quite clearly that the lamp is to be placed so that all can see it. In other words, we are called to be the lamp that all can see, and this means living lives of faith which run contrary to the values of the world in which we live. Whatever context we find ourselves in Jesus is inviting us to bear witness to our faith so that those around us can experience him through us. Remember what we said about the Bible that most people do not read it these days, but they do read us? This means that perhaps, for most people, their only experience of Christianity is what they discover in us. So, what should they find? What is the light we are called to be so that all may see?

Throughout the parables we find that at the core of Jesus's teaching is the revelation of the God of mercy, compassion, forgiveness, and love. There is tenderness, gentleness, and the overwhelming desire to comfort and heal all those who are suffering in any way. Here we find what Christ invites us to be. Here we discover our own vocation, which is to make real, in the here and now, that which Jesus, himself, came to bear witness to. Such an approach to life is a call to be different by living lives in accordance with the values of the Kingdom of Heaven not of the world. In a world dominated by celebrity the Christian is called to be anonymous. In a world dominated by power and strength the Christian is called to be weak. In a world dominated by money the Christian is called to be poor. In a world which turns its back on the voiceless and the marginalised the Christian is called to speak out for them. In a world dominated by achievement the Christian is called to bear witness to the cross. In a world which recognises and rewards success the Christian must herald the resurrection. Above and beyond all things the Christian must profess Christ crucified whilst at the same time recognising and serving him in all those who suffer. In this way the Christian becomes the lamp on the lampstand shining for all to see and yet in so doing it is Christ, himself, who is made known. This is the mission of every Christian and it must be the mission of his church too.

Eight:

Watch

Mark 13: 34-37

'Keep awake'

"It is like a man going on a journey, when he leaves home and puts his slaves in charge, each with his work, and commands the doorkeeper to be on the watch. Therefore, keep awake—for you do not know when the master of the house will come, in the evening, or at midnight, or at cockcrow, or at dawn, or else he may find you asleep when he comes suddenly. And what I say to you I say to all: Keep awake."

Looking around us, sometimes, it is easy to see the condition of the world in which we live and fall into a state of despondency. Jesus tells those who would follow him, *'To be in the world, but not of the world.'* but what does this mean? Many people these days do not believe in God and are often disillusioned with orthodox Christianity. At the same time, we are surrounded by secularism and materialism filling our minds and hearts with the need to be successful in the eyes of the world. Faced with such a prevailing culture what is the follower of Christ supposed to do?

This somewhat simple parable points us in the right direction. Jesus knew full well that he would not be with his disciples in the flesh for ever. Indeed, this passage comes right at the end of chapter thirteen before the plot to kill him really begins. So, with this in mind Jesus sets about preparing his disciples and all those who would come after them, to live lives of faith without his physical presence. Equally, of course, Jesus was aware that one day he would return to be with them again but when that would be was known only to his Father. Yet, Jesus also knew that his leaving would be gradual and something his disciples would find hard to accept. However, this event was inevitable, and the parable is part of the process whereby Jesus was teaching them and in turn us how to survive without him being physically present in the world.

What then is Jesus actually saying here which will have an effect on the way in which we live our lives of faith today? The parable tells us straight that a man is going on a journey and so must leave his home. Whilst he is away, he puts others in charge each with a specific task to perform, leaving the doorman to keep watch. However, there is a punchline to the parable because it is made clear that nobody knows when the homeowner will return. As a result, all those involved must stay on their guard otherwise when the master does return, he may well find them all asleep. When Jesus leaves, he does so by preparing beforehand, his disciples and in turn us for lives without him in the flesh. But he exhorts us to, '*Keep awake.*' But again, we may well ask, what does this mean?

Perhaps here we need to return to the world in which we live and make every effort not to be consumed by it. Without Jesus begin physically present our faith requires us to put all our trust in what, in fact, we cannot see. This involves not giving into the temptation to share in the unbelief we are often surrounded by but rather to look deeper for the mystery which surrounds our every waking moment. Once again, Jesus in this parable tells us that he will return but if we are to prepare effectively for this then we must resist the temptation to let ourselves be carried away by the values of the world around us. Not for the first time then Jesus exhorts us to stay awake and be committed to his values and the values of the Kingdom of Heaven. Eventually the time will come when Our Lord returns but not yet. In the meantime, the parables challenge us to see life and the world around us differently by asking fundamental questions about what it is to be human. To live lives of faith committed both to God and the needs of each other is the task given to us by Jesus in his absence, but we must always remain alert and be on the lookout for his coming.

Part Three:

Luke

'I will show you what someone is like who comes to me, hears my words, and acts on them. That one is like a man building a house, who dug deeply and laid the foundation on rock; when a flood arose, the river burst against that house but could not shake it, because it had been well built.'
(Luke 6:47-48)

One:

Stop No One

Luke 7:36 – 8:3

'Love Overwhelms Sin'

One of the Pharisees asked Jesus to eat with him, and he went into the Pharisee's house and took his place at the table. And a woman in the city, who was a sinner, having learned that he was eating in the Pharisee's house, brought an alabaster jar of ointment. She stood behind him at his feet, weeping, and began to bathe his feet with her tears and to dry them with her hair. Then she continued kissing his feet and anointing them with the ointment. Now when the Pharisee who had invited him saw it, he said to himself, "If this man were a prophet, he would have known who and what kind of woman this is who is touching him—that she is a sinner." Jesus spoke up and said to him, "Simon, I have something to say to you." "Teacher," he replied, "speak." "A certain creditor had two debtors: one owed five hundred denarii, and the other fifty. When they could not pay, he cancelled the debts for both of them. Now which of them will love him more?" Simon answered, "I suppose the one for whom he cancelled the greater debt." And Jesus said to him, "You have judged rightly." Then turning toward the woman, he said to Simon, "Do you see this woman? I entered your house; you gave me no water for my feet, but she has bathed my feet with her tears and dried them with her hair. You gave me no kiss, but from the time I came in she has not stopped kissing my feet. You did not anoint my head with oil, but she has anointed my feet with ointment. Therefore, I tell you, her sins, which were many, have been forgiven; hence she has shown great love. But the one to whom little is forgiven, loves little." Then he said to her, "Your sins are forgiven." But those who were at the table with him began to say among themselves, "Who is this who even forgives sins?" And he said to the woman, "Your faith has saved you; go in peace."

Soon afterwards he went on through cities and villages, proclaiming and bringing the good news of the kingdom of God. The twelve were with him, as well as some women who had been cured of evil spirits and infirmities: Mary, called Magdalene, from whom seven demons had gone out, and Joanna, the wife of Herod's steward Chuza, and Susanna, and many others, who provided for them out of their resources.

In exploring this parable, I am going to take a liberty by placing it within the context of the wider scene created by Luke. The parable itself is quite simple as described in Luke 7:41-43. Two men owed a sum of money to a money lender one owing much more than the other. As neither of them could afford to pay the debt back, the money lender cancelled them both. Jesus then asks, *'Now which of them will love him more?'* Simon replies, *'I suppose the one who had the bigger debt cancelled.'* We can only understand what Jesus says next by placing the parable within the broader context in which Jesus tells it. So here we go.

Jesus accepts an invitation given to him by a Pharisee called Simon, a religious leader, to attend a meal with him. This illustrates the important point that Jesus will bring the Gospel to all people; no one is to be left out. However, during the meal something happens which Simon did not, apparently, plan for. A woman turns up who may have been a prostitute with a large alabaster jar of perfume. She sits at Jesus's feet and weeps, her tears falling directly onto him. After this she wipes the tears away with her hair and kisses his feet before pouring the perfume onto them.

At this sight Simon would have been outraged and filled with contempt. Everyone knows who this woman is and what she does. Simon's reaction would have been to stop her, immediately, and remove her from the house. Yet what seems to be even more astonishing is that Jesus appears to allow and agree with this woman's outrageous behaviour. So, what is actually going on here then?

There can be little doubt that this woman knows who she is and what she has done. Yet there is a great need within her to express her love for Jesus in response to his forgiveness. To all those watching, this woman is a sinner and rejected by God because of her chosen way of life. As a result, the actions of Jesus, a good man, at least to all those present, is incomprehensible. By allowing himself to be touched by her it is tantamount to his own self-contamination or in other words he is making himself unclean and therefore a sinner too. Then the impossible happens, Jesus does something only God can do when he says to the woman, *'Your sins are forgiven.'* Here we are seeing at work, in Jesus, the loving tenderness and mercy of God such a feature in Luke's Gospel. Little wonder then that the people who witness this are astonished and say, *'Who is this who even forgives sins?'* Jesus, however, keeps his final words for the woman when he says to her, *'Your faith has saved you; go in peace.'*

When we go back to the parable, perhaps we are now in a much better position to understand its meaning. This is because the woman is forgiven much just like the person who owed the enormous amount in the parable.

Now we need to ground the meaning of this parable in everyday life. The first point to note, which is found in all the Gospels by the way, so it is incontestable, is the fact that Jesus accepted, understood, and embraced all those people who were rejected by the religious establishment of the day: tax collectors, prostitutes, the poor, the sick, the crippled, the diseased, the rejected, despised, unwanted and unloved. For this reason, Jesus was rejected, himself, by those same religious leaders. If God had rejected them so should everyone else was their message. Yet Jesus did the opposite, he assured them of God's love and God's forgiveness. What this encounter reveals though, and this is really important, is that it was the woman herself, who realised how much she needed forgiveness and how much she craved God's love.

So, what does this all mean for us then? Jesus was radical in the way he accepted those rejected by everyone else. The church and in turn all those who would follow Jesus have to be just as radical today, in our attitudes, if we are to be a true *light to the nations*. This means identifying all those whom society rejects and placing them at the very heart of who we are. Take for example women. Would it not be wonderful if the church today prioritised the importance and the role of women at all levels? Think of refugees, asylum seekers, migrant workers, the homeless and the destitute, all should find a home in the family of God. The divorced and separated, those of a different sexual orientation, or anyone living on the margins of society must be embraced by the people of God today. Should not the church in whatever form it takes be a leading voice in society, shouting from the rooftops if necessary, on behalf of all those who have no voice? Should not each and every one of us, calling ourselves Christian, be constantly examining our attitudes on anyone pushed to the margins of society by asking, *'What can I do?'*

There must be a place where anyone who feels they are unwanted, rejected, despised or unloved can turn to and find acceptance. There is such a place, in fact and it is called the church. Finally, what can such people hope to find amongst us that they simply will not find anywhere else? The answer, in the name of Jesus, whom we are called to know, and serve is the mercy, compassion, forgiveness and love of God.

Two:

The Good Samaritan

Luke 10:25-37

'What must I do?'

Just then a lawyer stood up to test Jesus. "Teacher," he said, "what must I do to inherit eternal life?" He said to him, "What is written in the law? What do you read there?" He answered, "You shall love the Lord your God with all your heart, and with all your soul, and with all your strength, and with all your mind; and your neighbour as yourself." And he said to him, "You have given the right answer; do this, and you will live."

But wanting to justify himself, he asked Jesus, "And who is my neighbour?" Jesus replied, "A man was going down from Jerusalem to Jericho, and fell into the hands of robbers, who stripped him, beat him, and went away, leaving him half dead. Now by chance a priest was going down that road; and when he saw him, he passed by on the other side. So likewise, a Levite, when he came to the place and saw him, passed by on the other side. But a Samaritan while traveling came near him; and when he saw him, he was moved with pity. He went to him and bandaged his wounds, having poured oil and wine on them. Then he put him on his own animal, brought him to an inn, and took care of him. The next day he took out two denarii, gave them to the innkeeper, and said, 'Take care of him; and when I come back, I will repay you whatever more you spend.' Which of these three, do you think, was a neighbour to the man who fell into the hands of the robbers?" He said, "The one who showed him mercy." Jesus said to him, "Go and do likewise."

I wonder how we would answer the question, *'Who do you love and who don't you love?'* or putting it another way, *'How do we decide who to love?'* Are such questions, however, even Christian, after all what, in fact, is love? The parable of The Good Samaritan serves to provide deep insight into questions such as these and in doing so illuminates the way in which we should live out our Christian lives on a day-to-day basis.

A teacher of the religious law asks Jesus a question as they discuss how to attain eternal life. Jesus, however, turns the question on its head by asking in response, *'What does the law say on this?'* The young man, perhaps, eager to illustrate his expertise replies immediately with, *'Love of God and neighbour.'* Jesus confirms his reply but the lawyer, in front of the gathered crowed now pushes his legalistic approach even further by demanding that Jesus defines who his neighbour is. At this stage it is important to note how rigid and inflexible the young man is by demanding that the law of God be clearly defined.

As a result, Jesus changes tactics completely. His mission is to reveal the compassion, mercy, and love of God by confronting the suffering experienced by people. Such an approach takes priority over any law. So, Jesus now tells him a parable which confronts a legalistic, inflexible, and rigid approach to God and replaces it with loving service to anyone who needs it.

A man is on a journey from Jerusalem to Jericho, but we know nothing about him. On the way he is attacked by robbers who leave him stripped and half-dead by the side of the road. All we now know is that he is a fellow human being in desperate need of help. At this point a priest enters the scene, a man devoted to God but who primarily works in the temple. He does not see it as his duty or responsibility to help this stranger because his life is devoted to worship. What we are seeing here is a complete lack of compassion and mercy, characteristics Jesus always associates with his Father. Perhaps the lawyer should take note but, of course, Jesus is not finished yet.

The Levite who now comes along serves only to confirm the behaviour and the attitude of the priest when he does, exactly, the same thing. What such actions reveal is the kind of attitude revealed by the young lawyer who asked Jesus the original question. What then do the three men have in common? Firstly, they see themselves as experts or professionals when it comes to God and how people should follow him. Secondly, they live privileged lives cut off from those who must struggle to survive. And thirdly they have reduced faith to the following of a set of rigid, inflexible laws. Where might you ask is God in all of this?

Jesus on the other hand confronts them with something completely different; God who is intimately involved in every aspect of our lives. You see Jesus reveals the God of mercy, compassion, forgiveness, and love. If the law and sacred worship refuses to recognise this fundamental truth, then they ultimately drive people away from him. How can it be right that adherence to the law can prevent people from responding to suffering in any of its forms? What then, according to Jesus, takes priority over the law and worship? The answer is compassion.

It is a Samaritan, or a foreigner, who refuses to pass by on the other side of the road. He is not a lawyer, nor does he worship in the temple, in fact he is not even a Jew. Yet he sees what the other two refuse to see, a fellow human being in need. His response now resonates with everything Jesus came to reveal about God, *'he was moved with compassion.'* In fact, he asks no questions about faith or religion, he simply acts, and his heart goes out to this man he finds by the side of the road. This is the kind of behaviour Jesus says is expected from those who would reflect something of the nature and being of God.

When he comes to the end of the parable Jesus turns to the young and enthusiastic lawyer and asks him a question, *'Which of the three, do you think, was a neighbour to the man who fell into the hands of the robbers?'* His response is by now not only obvious but turns his original legalistic approach on its head, *'The one who showed him mercy.'* Jesus now only has one more thing to say not just to the lawyer but to you and me and all those who would follow him, and it is this, *'Go and do the same yourself.'*

As I wrote this reflection something occurred to me and I will finish by sharing it with you. The young lawyer answered correctly when Jesus asked him, *'What does the law tell you about inheriting eternal life?'* *'Love God and love your neighbour as yourself,'* means to feel and experience what God feels, which Jesus tells us, ultimately, is compassion, for all those who suffer. Yet feelings by themselves are not enough they must be expressed in action.

Three:

Ask, Seek, and Knock

Luke 11:1-13

'Trust'

He was praying in a certain place, and after he had finished, one of his disciples said to him, "Lord, teach us to pray, as John taught his disciples." He said to them, "When you pray, say:

Father, hallowed be your name.
Your kingdom come.
Give us each day our daily bread.
And forgive us our sins,
for we ourselves forgive everyone indebted to us.
And do not bring us to the time of trial."

And he said to them, "Suppose one of you has a friend, and you go to him at midnight and say to him, 'Friend, lend me three loaves of bread; a friend of mine has arrived, and I have nothing to set before him.' And he answers from within, 'Do not bother me; the door has already been locked, and my children are with me in bed; I cannot get up and give you anything.' I tell you, even though he will not get up and give him anything because he is his friend, at least because of his persistence he will get up and give him whatever he needs.

"So, I say to you, Ask, and it will be given you; search, and you will find; knock, and the door will be opened for you. For everyone who asks receives, and everyone who searches finds, and for everyone who knocks, the door will be opened. Is there anyone among you who, if your child asks for[e] a fish, will give a snake instead of a fish? Or if the child asks for an egg, will give a scorpion? If you then, who are evil, know how to give good gifts to your children, how much more will the heavenly Father give the Holy Spirit to those who ask him?"

Sometimes I think it can be really helpful to understand the meaning of a parable by imagining a conversation between Jesus and his disciples. This approach is something I am going to apply to Luke 11:1-13. There can be little doubt that the disciples on numerous occasions would have seen Jesus at prayer. After one such period, his disciples turn to him and ask, '*Lord, teach us to pray, as John taught his disciples.*' Jesus's response is to offer them the Lord's Prayer.

As Jesus journeyed with his disciples throughout the region of Galilee there would have been times when they were turned away and were not made to feel welcome. During such periods it is not hard for us to imagine that the twelve may well have become disheartened and discouraged. It was in these moments that Jesus would have urged them to keep going placing all their trust in God. Perhaps the disciples envied their Lord desiring to share in the kind of intimacy he had with his Father. Of course, this is exactly what Jesus wanted for them too. It may well have been within this kind of context that Jesus told a parable about a friend who approaches someone at midnight asking for bread. However, they are too tired, tucked up in bed and in essence cannot be bothered to come to their aid. Yet Jesus insists that, in the end, they will get up and give their friend what he requests, simply because he asks.

This now enables Jesus to instruct his disciples further on their relationship with God, '*Ask and it will be given to you; seek and you will find; knock and the door will be opened to you.*' Jesus is, in fact, sharing his own experience with his father when he goes even further by saying: '*for everyone who asks receives; he who seeks finds; and to him who knocks, the door will be opened.*'

To apply this to our own lives today and to that of the church we have to ask ourselves, '*What do we do in times of crisis?*' Is our first reaction to *trust* in God as Jesus invites us to or do, we panic and lose heart as, perhaps, the disciples were tempted to do within the context of this parable? Jesus makes it clear that there are three ways forward each of which is designed to express our *trust* in God.

Firstly, we have to be prepared to *ask* by knowing and believing that we are in desperate need of something we cannot achieve by ourselves. Do we really know our need for God? Are we the kind of person who is simply too proud to ask for help? Do we find admitting to weakness too much of a threat? Do we look for help from other sources first because we find it impossible to rely totally on God? Is the world, therefore, a safer bet when we look for help and protection?

What about *seeking* then? The first point to make is that it is not the same as *asking* because it suggests action of some kind. What then does Jesus suggest we actively look for? The answer has to be because it is there throughout the whole of his ministry, the *Kingdom of God.* This Kingdom is radically different to the world in which we live because it is one built on mercy, compassion, forgiveness, and love. This is what Jesus urges us to seek with all our hearts. This is the foundation upon which our faith and that of the church is built but it starts with our *trust* in God, and it *seeks* justice for all. This is the Gospel which needs to be offered to the world through lives of faith which make a difference not just to ourselves and the church but to all those who are unwanted, rejected, despised and unloved by the world today.

Finally, we come to the *knock* which in essence is a *cry* from the deepest depths of our soul to God our father. Yet we do so believing, that he cannot only hear us but out of his love for us will always respond. Many of us are reluctant to use the word *cry* because, in the eyes of the world, it makes us appear weak. Yet Jesus, alone and dying *cried* out to his father from the cross and Saint Paul was able to say, *'For when I am weak, then I am strong.'* (2 Corinthians 12:10) In this parable Jesus is strengthening our faith and that of the church by exhorting us to place all our trust in God. Thus, our first port of call, in times of crisis and distress, should always be to turn to our Father knowing and believing that he will always respond to our cries for help out of his overwhelming love.

Four:

Greed

Luke 12:13-21

'What shall I do?'

Someone in the crowd said to him, "Teacher, tell my brother to divide the family inheritance with me." But he said to him, "Friend, who set me to be a judge or arbitrator over you?" And he said to them, "Take care! Be on your guard against all kinds of greed; for one's life does not consist in the abundance of possessions." Then he told them a parable: "The land of a rich man produced abundantly. And he thought to himself, 'What should I do, for I have no place to store my crops?' Then he said, 'I will do this: I will pull down my barns and build larger ones, and there I will store all my grain and my goods. And I will say to my soul, Soul, you have ample goods laid up for many years; relax, eat, drink, be merry.' But God said to him, 'You fool! This very night your life is being demanded of you. And the things you have prepared, whose will they be?' So, it is with those who store up treasures for themselves but are not rich toward God."

In all of these parables we need to have the courage not only to apply them to ourselves but to the world in which we live. It is my belief that the Gospels are nothing less than a new literary genre and, therefore, need to be read as such. As a result, they are both timeless and contain the words of life. This is why they continue to challenge the standards, values, and morals of our modern world.

I think we all know that there are rich and powerful people in the world today just as there was in the time of Jesus. Even today there are those who see riches as a blessing from God. The Gospels, in fact, are full of incidences whereby the rich and powerful exploit the poor, all of which are endorsed by their religious leaders. Time and time again, however, Jesus makes something abundantly clear, *'It is hard for someone rich man to enter the kingdom of Heaven, it is easier for a camel to fit through the eye of a needle than for someone rich to enter the kingdom of Heaven.'* (Matthew 19:23-

24) So what are we to make of this particular parable and what is it saying both to us, the church, and the world in which we all live today?

We have a rich lander owner who has a bumper harvest. Indeed, his crop is so great that he does not have enough barns to contain it all so, *'What shall I do'* he asks? At this point we need to stop and reflect on this person's main concerns in life. He appears to have no family because they are not mentioned, neither are his friends, neighbours or the poor labourers who work the land for him. So, the only person he is really thinking about is himself.

What are the dangers in this attitude to life is Jesus warning us about here? What do we need to consider when reflecting on our own values and morals when it comes to wealth accumulation? The suggestion being made in this parable is that the only thing the landowner is concerned about is his own wealth. This then has a direct impact on the way in which he lives his life and his relationship with others. The question then arises does this make him more or less human? The conclusion Jesus wants us to come to is a resounding, no! We can tell what state of mind the landowner is in when he states quite clearly, *I will tear down my barns and build bigger ones, and there I will store all my grain and my goods. And I'll say to myself, "You have plenty of good things laid up for many years. Take it easy, eat, drink and be merry.'* In many ways this is the climax of the story because the man appears to have sorted his life out and assured his wealth driven future. As a result, he can sit back, enjoy life, and relax.

So, what can we learn from the parable so far and how can we apply it to our own lives today? Driven by greed, the landowner has sorted out his own life, he is in charge and the time has come, perhaps, to retire and enjoy his amassed fortune. However, it is at that point that God intervenes, *'You fool! This very night your life will be demanded from you. Then who will get what you prepared for yourself?'* What then does this say about the landowner's life and his search for prosperity and security based, exclusively, on his own efforts?

Let us think now about his obsession to build bigger barns so that his bumper harvest can be accommodated. How does this help him become a better human being? Where is his concern not only for his labourers who helped him achieve his financial goals but also for those less fortunate than himself? There is no mention in this parable at all about the landowner's, compassion, empathy, concern, or love. Where is his sense of generosity and obligation to help people who are far less fortunate than he is? Instead, what we discover is a person whose humanity has diminished. As a result, he has allowed his obsession with wealth to define who he is, devoid of a family, friends, or neighbours. Indeed, all he has is his fortune and the rest of the world, including the poor are an irrelevance. How sad is that? Yet, in the end everything he has is taken from him.

The meaning of this parable is a powerful reminder to the modern world of what defines us as human beings. Are we, in fact, defined by our obsession to accumulate more and more wealth to the detriment of the poor? These words of Jesus are addressed not just to us as individuals but also to the church, banks, financial institutions, the rich and the powerful all over the world. Where does our real security lie? What happens to use when all we really care about is generating more and more profit to be enjoyed by fewer and fewer people? What about our obligation to help those less fortunate than ourselves? How can it be right to surround ourselves with a blanket of wealth, insulating us from suffering humanity, with an attitude of indifference to the cries of the poor? If we look into the mirror is this what we see or as with the landowner in the parable are we simply just too afraid to look? So, God says to us, *'You fool!'*

Deep within each and every single one of us speaks the voice of God urging us not to be cruel, not to be indifferent, and not to live our lives in such a *foolish* way. The church and all those who would walk in the footsteps of Jesus are invited by him to live lives motivated not by personal and institutional financial gain but rather by compassion for all those in need. When that defines our humanity, then that is the day when everything changes, and the values of the Gospel become clearly visible for all to see.

Five:

Where was God?

Luke 13:1-9

'Where were you?'

At that very time there were some present who told him about the Galileans whose blood Pilate had mingled with their sacrifices. He asked them, "Do you think that because these Galileans suffered in this way, they were worse sinners than all other Galileans? No, I tell you; but unless you repent, you will all perish as they did. Or those eighteen who were killed when the tower of Siloam fell on them—do you think that they were worse offenders than all the others living in Jerusalem? No, I tell you; but unless you repent, you will all perish just as they did."

Then he told this parable: "A man had a fig tree planted in his vineyard; and he came looking for fruit on it and found none. So, he said to the gardener, 'See here! For three years I have come looking for fruit on this fig tree, and still, I find none. Cut it down! Why should it be wasting the soil?' He replied, 'Sir, let it alone for one more year, until I dig around it and put manure on it. If it bears fruit next year, well and good; but if not, you can cut it down.'"

This is one of those parables, which if I am perfectly honest, at first sight I struggle with in terms of understanding its meaning. For this reason, I have placed it within the wider context of the whole passage from Luke.

So, a man plants a fig tree and leaves it to be looked after by someone else. After three years of care the tree still fails to produce fruit so the owner decides to cut it down. At this point, his servant intercedes on behalf of the tree arguing that, if after one more year of his careful care, the tree still fails to bear fruit it can then be cut down. Or in other words the servant is asking the owner to give the tree one more chance to produce fruit. What can this possibly mean?

Firstly, let us look at what happens in the passage immediately prior to the parable. A group of unknown people approach Jesus telling him that under the orders of Pilate some Galileans have been killed and their blood mixed with that of animals being sacrificed and offered to God. Why did these people tell Jesus this? What motivated them to come to him? What were they expecting his reaction to be? What were they hoping for? Did they, perhaps, think that such people must have done something to offend God to warrant such a horrific death? If this was not the case then how come if the victims were, in fact, innocent, would God allow such an awful thing to take place in the temple?

The response of Jesus to this appears, at first sight, to be quite strange. He tells them about another set of events, which again took place in Jerusalem and involved the death of eighteen people who were crushed when a tower close to the pool of Siloam collapsed. What, however, does all this mean and how are the two incidents connected? Perhaps, Jesus is making the point that in both cases those who died were no less or no more guilty than anyone else living in Jerusalem. As a result, the section finishes with these words, *'Unless you repent, you too will perish.'* In other words, Jesus is suggesting that they should take the opportunity of recognising who it is standing before them and change their ways; just like the fig tree was given one more year to bear fruit.

Here, Jesus clearly rejects any suggestion that disasters are to be interpreted as punishments sent from God, which was, in fact, one of the prevailing views of the day. In this way, Jesus also makes something abundantly clear, that any teaching that even suggests God punishes sin by sending sickness, poverty or death is wrong. So, what does all this mean then? How are we to make sense out of the disasters which not only come our way in life but, which very often strike also at the heart of those people least able to cope? How can we now make sense out of it all?

When disaster strikes, no matter what it is, we might be tempted to react by asking, *'where was God? How can a loving God allow such things to happen? Why doesn't this all-powerful God do something?'* Indeed, in my visits to schools these are the questions young people immediately fire at me when we are discussing natural disasters.

Yet Jesus is teaching us that these are the wrong questions, instead we should be asking ourselves, *'where was I?'* Or putting it another way, we should let God ask us, *'where were you?'* In this way such incidences become opportunities to change our lives, to become more compassionate, to become more human, and to become more like Christ.

When we are confronted with any kind of disaster but particularly those which impact on the poorest people on earth, we should be challenged to ask a range of uncomfortable questions of ourselves. *Why are some people so desperately poor and therefore least able to cope when natural disasters strike? Why are there such inequalities in the world resulting in untold human suffering? Why, when there are enough resources, including food, to go around we simply refuse to share? Why do we allow or turn a blind eye to so much human suffering and misery?* The answers to all these questions, which we may not like, comes from God, *'where were you?'* This then is the driving force behind the parable, God gives us all one more chance to do something. The challenge is to discover God in that place where we never thought of looking for him, in all those victims, in all those who suffer and in all those who cry out to us in pain.

This is how Saint Mother Teresa put it:

*'I used to pray that God
would feed the hungry, or will do this or that,
but now I pray that he will guide me
to do whatever I'm supposed to do,
what I can do.
I used to pray for answers,
but now I'm praying for strength.
I used to believe that prayer changes things,
but now I know that prayer changes us
and we change things.'*

If the parable of the fig tree teaches us anything, it is that God always gives us another chance to act but there is not an option to do nothing.

Six:

The Cost of Discipleship

Luke 14:25-33

'Prepare, listen and discern'

Now large crowds were traveling with him; and he turned and said to them, "Whoever comes to me and does not hate father and mother, wife and children, brothers, and sisters, yes, and even life itself, cannot be my disciple. Whoever does not carry the cross and follow me cannot be my disciple. For which of you, intending to build a tower, does not first sit down and estimate the cost, to see whether he has enough to complete it? Otherwise, when he has laid a foundation and is not able to finish, all who see it will begin to ridicule him, saying, 'This fellow began to build and was not able to finish.' Or what king, going out to wage war against another king, will not sit down first and consider whether he is able with ten thousand to oppose the one who comes against him with twenty thousand? If he cannot, then, while the other is still far away, he sends a delegation and asks for the terms of peace. So therefore, none of you can become my disciple if you do not give up all your possessions."

I have taken the title for this reflection from a book by Dietrich Bonhoeffer, *'The Cost of Discipleship'* (SCM Press; New edition 31 August 2015). It is a work I have always found hugely challenging, and it is well worth a read if you would like to know more about how Bonhoeffer sees what it means to be a disciple of Christ set against the regime of the Nazis in his own country of Germany.

In this parable Jesus makes something abundantly clear, that before anyone undertakes a major project it is prudent to make sure you have the resources to complete it. If not, then you run the risk of failure and ridicule. He then sets out two examples which serve to make his point. Firstly, someone wanting to build a tower to protect their vineyard would be wise to make sure that they are able to complete the job before starting it. If not, then their failure would invite only humour from the neighbours. Secondly, any king would make sure he had enough troops to win a battle before starting one otherwise it may well end in defeat.

Is Jesus merely suggesting caution here or is there something deeper at work? Perhaps, the point Jesus is making both to his disciples and the church today is that the mission he is entrusting to them and in turn to us is so great it merits deep reflection before anyone commits themselves to it. Putting it another way, it is a bit like Jesus asking, *'Do you really know what you are undertaking, or do you really understand what it is I am asking of you?'* Before we say *'yes'* to this question, we are being urged to take the time to stop and think things through. In this sense, it is like a warning urging us to delve deep into our hearts to discover whether this is something we can really commit our lives to or not. Hence, we are not to take the mission given to us by Christ himself lightly. This then makes for extremely powerful stuff.

So, going back to the parable itself and being rather practical, what resources do we need if we are to accept Jesus's invitation to be part of his mission for the salvation of the world? Perhaps, the first point to note is that this is something we cannot do by ourselves. Rather we need to work in partnership with one another working out what needs to be done and how the project can be resourced. This inevitably requires us to listen to each other, work together and discern collectively what actions should be taken. Here careful and cohesive planning is the key. However, we must never forget one essential ingredient to this process and that is to spend more time both listening to the Gospel and reflecting, inspired by the grace of the Holy Spirit, on exactly what Christ is calling us to do.

One of the greatest challenges facing the church today is how to respond to the needs of the ever-changing modern world. As I write this reflection Pope Francis is inviting the Catholic Church all over the world to engage in a listening process, involving all the people of God, to discern what Christ is calling the Church to be in the modern world. This process of listening and discernment with the people of God working together is called co-responsibility, ultimately finding expression in what Pope Francis calls the *synodal way.* The challenge is to discover new ways of being the church for all people, to promote new charisms and therefore develop fresh ways of being authentic witnesses to Christ in the world today. Yet in amongst all this Jesus, as we can clearly see in the parable above, urges us to know what we are planning for. The world is changing rapidly, and we must be conscious of this in terms of the environment, social and political climate, and the ever-increasing gap between the rich and the poor. What has the Gospel of Jesus Christ to say to such a world? There can be little doubt that people are feeling increasingly isolated from each other with the continued increase of technology and social media, resulting in an explosion of mental health issues. How can the church and the language of faith inspire such a generation who feel increasingly disillusioned with orthodox religion? Facing such overwhelming challenges, how does the church need to change to speak and engage with people who do not know Christ and his great love for them? How can the church use the language of God's love to inspire a new generation to co-operate with the Holy Spirit so that the whole world might be transformed by his grace?

Jesus simply invites us to sit down and work together, perhaps to rediscover a truth that we can all too easily forget, that he lives and works in and through us. Now more than ever, the church is facing the challenge to be in the world but not of the world, called to be *a light to the nations* of God's love for all people and to point to Jesus Christ as the source of all *our hope and all our joy*. How we do that effectively is, perhaps, still a work in progress.

Seven:

The Lost Son – Part I

Luke 15:1-32

'Father help us find our way'

Now all the tax collectors and sinners were coming near to listen to him. And the Pharisees and the scribes were grumbling and saying, "This fellow welcomes sinners and eats with them."

So, he told them this parable: "Which one of you, having a hundred sheep and losing one of them, does not leave the ninety-nine in the wilderness and go after the one that is lost until he finds it? When he has found it, he lays it on his shoulders and rejoices. And when he comes home, he calls together his friends and neighbours, saying to them, 'Rejoice with me, for I have found my sheep that was lost.' Just so, I tell you, there will be more joy in heaven over one sinner who repents than over ninety-nine righteous persons who need no repentance.

"Or what woman having ten silver coins, if she loses one of them, does not light a lamp, sweep the house, and search carefully until she finds it? When she has found it, she calls together her friends and neighbours, saying, 'Rejoice with me, for I have found the coin that I had lost.' Just so, I tell you, there is joy in the presence of the angels of God over one sinner who repents."

Then Jesus said, "There was a man who had two sons. The younger of them said to his father, 'Father, give me the share of the property that will belong to me.' So, he divided his property between them. A few days later the younger son gathered all he had and travelled to a distant country, and there he squandered his property in dissolute living. When he had spent everything, a severe famine took place throughout that country, and he began to be in need. So, he went and hired himself out to one of the citizens of that country, who sent him to his fields to feed the pigs. He would gladly have filled himself with[c] the pods that the pigs were eating; and no one gave him anything. But when he came to himself, he said, 'How many of my father's hired hands have bread enough and to spare, but here I am dying of hunger! I will get up and go to my father, and I will say to him, "Father, I have sinned against heaven and before you; I am no longer worthy to be called your son; treat me like one of your hired hands."' So, he set off and went to his father. But while he was still far off, his father saw him and was filled with compassion; he ran and put his arms around him and kissed him. Then the son said to him, 'Father, I have sinned against heaven and before you; I am no longer worthy to be called your son.' But the father said to his slaves, 'Quickly, bring out a robe—the best one—and put it on him; put a ring on his finger and sandals on his feet. And get the fatted calf and kill it and let us eat and celebrate; for this son of mine was dead and is alive again; he was lost and is found!' And they began to celebrate.

"Now his elder son was in the field; and when he came and approached the house, he heard music and dancing. He called one of the slaves and asked what was going on. He replied, 'Your brother has come, and your father has killed the fatted calf, because he has got him back safe and sound.' Then he became angry and refused to go in. His father came out and began to plead with him. But he answered his father, 'Listen! For all these years I have been working like a slave for you, and I have never disobeyed your command; yet you have never given me even a young goat so that I might celebrate with my friends. But when this son of yours came back, who has devoured your property with prostitutes, you killed the fatted calf for him!' Then the father said to him, 'Son, you are always with me, and all that is mine is yours. But we had to celebrate and rejoice, because this brother of yours was dead and has come to life; he was lost and has been found.'"

There is no other parable like *The Lost Son* in the Gospels which invites us to reflect on ourselves, our faith and the nature and being of God. Indeed, in many ways the parable of the *Lost Son* is perfect for delving deeper into the mission of the church in the modern world. Hence, once again, it is crucial when calling to mind Pope Francis's invitation to Catholics all over the world to listen to each other and work together, if a way forward is to be found to speak to those who have either never heard the Gospel of Jesus Christ or who have drifted away from it.

If we are to truly engage and wrestle with the meaning of this parable then we need to interpret it within the context of the modern world. Right from the beginning the younger son sets his stall out when he goes to his father and says, *'Give me my share of the estate.'* In essence, he is demanding his freedom now because he is unwilling to wait until his father dies. Perhaps, surprisingly, the father gives in to his son's request straight away. This reveals a simple truth, that God will not coerce, manipulate, or control us, rather he gives us the freedom to choose our own path in life. Yet is this not also an accurate reflection of modern society, at least in the west? Many, dare I say the majority, have rejected God seeing belief in him as an irrelevance having no impact on their lives whatsoever. Indeed, society merely reflects this apathy or indifference by very often ridiculing or distancing itself from Christianity. God, however, remains silent, we are free to choose our own way just as the younger son did in the parable.

The drama now takes the actions of the younger son a stage further when he moves as far away as possible from his father. But what he does not know, is that his father never stopped loving him, waiting every day for his wayward son to return. In fact, the heart of the father went out to his son as he missed him, yearning for him to come back. So, in truth, the father went with his son and stayed with him even though he never realised it. The same is true today, that although people, by and large, are leaving God and the church, he will never leave us simply because he loves us more than we could ever know.

In the far distant land, the son now lives in, life for him appears to be good or so it seems. He can enjoy his freedom without reference to his father and lives as though he were dead. There is, however, a break-down in his moral behaviour and things come to a dramatic end when the money runs out. He is now forced to work with pigs', animals identified by God in the Law as being unclean. This is how low his life has sunk. Hungry, cold, and homeless he now laments his tragic situation summed up in his words, *'Here I am starving to death.'*

We have now reached, in fact, the crucial part of the parable, in so far as the younger son must realise something for himself. What does he yearn for? What does he desire more than anything else? What does he need if he is to survive? The answer to all these questions is, in fact, something he had always possessed but never realised, the love of his father. Looking at things from a slightly different perspective, for the younger son freedom was not, in fact, what he thought it would be. Eventually he had to realise something for himself, that he had a need or a longing deep within his own heart that only his father's love could fulfil. A father who had never, unknown to him of course, stopped loving him.

What brings him back ultimately is the face of his father. Discovering the emptiness within the depths of his own heart he finds another form of freedom which can only be enjoyed close to his father. He calls to mind his real home overflowing with food, kindness and love and thinks, *'they have food to spare and here am I starving to death.'* Now he knows for himself that this is where he needs to be, close to his father, in his father's house and he decides to return home. The crucial point here though is that just as he chose to leave in the first place, now he is choosing, for himself, to return.

We now need to bring ourselves back to the modern world. How can the church engage, effectively, with all those who have either never heard the Gospel or who have drifted away from it? What can the church do to speak to people who are disillusioned with orthodox Christianity because of its perceived corruption and failure to be an authentic witness to Christ? Perhaps, the starting point is for all of us, who call ourselves Christian, to understand the way in which Jesus reveals his father. In the parable what does the father do? Jesus puts it like this, *'He ran to meet his son, threw his arms around him and kissed him.'* In this way we are drawn into an understanding of what God is really like. He seeks only to love us, to embrace us and yes, to kiss us. He loves us more than we could ever know or comprehend, and Jesus reduces all of this to a parable. This is the image of God we need to rediscover and offer to a waiting world, the God of compassion, mercy, and love. It is ironic, is it not, that the young son found his true freedom not far from his father but rather in his father's arms. This simple language is what Jesus used to describe his Father and it is something we all need to find again. Perhaps, the key though, in speaking of God to the modern world is to make these words live in our own lives and in our own churches. Can we be merciful just like the Father, can we be compassionate just like the Father, can we forgive just like the Father and above all can we love just like the Father? Because if we could do all these things then maybe, just maybe, the modern world would, sit up, listen, and return home.

Eight:

The Father's Love or The Lost Son Part II

Luke 15:1-3, 11-32

'Some uncomfortable home truths'

Now all the tax collectors and sinners were coming near to listen to him. And the Pharisees and the scribes were grumbling and saying, "This fellow welcomes sinners and eats with them."

So, he told them this parable:

Then Jesus said, "There was a man who had two sons. The younger of them said to his father, 'Father, give me the share of the property that will belong to me.' So, he divided his property between them. A few days later the younger son gathered all he had and travelled to a distant country, and there he squandered his property in dissolute living. When he had spent everything, a severe famine took place throughout that country, and he began to be in need. So, he went and hired himself out to one of the citizens of that country, who sent him to his fields to feed the pigs. He would gladly have filled himself with[b] the pods that the pigs were eating; and no one gave him anything. But when he came to himself, he said, 'How many of my father's hired hands have bread enough and to spare, but here I am dying of hunger! I will get up and go to my father, and I will say to him, "Father, I have sinned against heaven and before you; I am no longer worthy to be called your son; treat me like one of your hired hands."' So, he set off and went to his father. But while he was still far off, his father saw him and was filled with compassion; he ran and put his arms around him and kissed him. Then the son said to him, 'Father, I have sinned against heaven and before you; I am no longer worthy to be called your son.' But the father said to his slaves, 'Quickly, bring out a robe—the best one—and put it on him; put a ring on his finger and sandals on his feet. And get the fatted calf and kill it and let us eat and celebrate; for this son of mine was dead and is alive again; he was lost and is found!' And they began to celebrate.

"Now his elder son was in the field; and when he came and approached the house, he heard music and dancing. He called one of the slaves and asked what was going on. He replied, 'Your brother has come, and your father has killed the fatted calf, because he has got him back safe and sound.' Then he

became angry and refused to go in. His father came out and began to plead with him. But he answered his father, 'Listen! For all these years I have been working like a slave for you, and I have never disobeyed your command; yet you have never given me even a young goat so that I might celebrate with my friends. But when this son of yours came back, who has devoured your property with prostitutes, you killed the fatted calf for him!' Then the father[d] said to him, 'Son, you are always with me, and all that is mine is yours. But we had to celebrate and rejoice, because this brother of yours was dead and has come to life; he was lost and has been found.'"

Such is the power and importance of this parable I have decided to provide two reflections on it. Indeed, the church deems it so crucial to our understanding of God that it is read to the faithful twice in Cycle C of that liturgical year. Yet it can make for an uncomfortable read and it is easy to neglect the importance of the father and his love for both sons, which of course reflects his love for us.

In this reflection I am, however, going to concentrate on the older of the two sons. He is the one who stays by his father's side, the faithful one who cannot for the life of him understand the attitude of his younger brother. When he hears of his wayward brother's return his initial reaction is bafflement as he learns of the party being given by his father to celebrate the reunion. However, this soon turns to anger and frustration when we are told, *'He became angry and refused to go in to join the feasting.'* He was the one who had remained loyal, staying by his father's side for all these years and this is how he is repaid.

At this point let us turn to the father summoned by his older son who is refusing to join in with all the festivities. He greets his son only with love and assures him that everything he owns is his too. The father reveals his nature of loving humility willing to treat both of his sons in the same way regardless of the mistakes they might make in life. There is no anger or frustration in the father, his words and manner speak only of compassion. Perhaps, it is this which breaks the older son because now he must let his father know how he really feels. In anger and frustration everything now pours out of him, how all these years he had stayed by his father's side working hard on the land. He had done everything he thought his father had wanted him to do unlike, of course, his younger brother who had done exactly the opposite. So why the welcome back? Why the party? Why all the celebration and festivities? Why reward wrongdoing? It is not fair, it is not just, it is not right, and it does not make sense! What the older son is really saying, is demanding from his father what he believes he deserves, what is his by right, what he has earned. Yet amid all this the one thing he has failed to learn is how to love, like his father.

Most of the commentaries and reflections on this parable invite us to identify with the younger son, the sinner who repents and comes home but here I want us to concentrate our attention on the older brother. He knows how to work the land, to do what is expected of him and to stay by his father's side but he fails to understand how to love. To this end, he cannot comprehend how his father can still love his younger brother who abandoned them and squandered half of the family's estate. To him this just does not make any sense. As a result, he cannot welcome his brother back nor can he forgive him, in fact the implication is that he does not want to have anything to do with his brother at all. If you return to the parable for a moment, have a look at the ending because it might surprise you. There is no resolution. We do not know what happens next and Jesus obviously wants us to reflect deeply on that.

This now brings us back to the church in the modern world and to the initiative of Pope Francis who has invited the people of God to listen and discern together as to what the Holy Spirit is calling the church to be and do, given the times in which we live. This is perhaps where we need to be courageous and listen to *'some uncomfortable home truths.'* What if we, as the church, identify with the older son in the parable and are being looked at by the modern world, what do they see? Well first, we believe we live close to God and are doing what he wants us to do. We have stayed loyal to the church and have not left, unlike most people.

But what are we doing? The parable reveals that to stay close to God means to be like him filled with his mercy, compassion, forgiveness, and love for all people. This then leads to asking some rather uncomfortable questions such as, how welcoming are we as Christian communities? How willing are we to reach out to those who have either left the church or who have never seen themselves as part of it? Are we comfortable in encouraging people to question when they have doubts and walk alongside them, journeying together in search of the God of infinite love? How aware are we of the barriers we often put up which discourage people from approaching us because they are unable to see in our lives the God who turns no one away? How obsessed are we with maintaining what we have rather than with what we are called to be?

The parable teaches us something profound about God which Jesus invites us to reflect in our lives of faith both as the church and as individuals. That God loves all people equally, without exception and that he has no favourites. That God's love cannot be earned because it is given as a gift. That God's love is overwhelmingly generous and that once given it will never be taken back. That God only knows how to be merciful, compassionate, forgiving, and loving. If we could somehow live lives like that then the world would be changed. If the church could bear authentic witness to such a Gospel, then people would come.

Yet we spend so much of our time almost doing the opposite. We give people labels and identify them as either for us or against us. Think about it, we talk about practicing and lapsed Catholics, conservative and liberal Catholics, believers, and unbelievers, hence people are either in or out, part of us or not part us, one of us or not one of us, even good Catholics, and bad Catholics. Will we ever learn?

I have called this reflection *'The Father's Love,'* because ultimately this is the core meaning of the parable. God does not label us or differentiate between us because he simply loves *us*. And when I say he loves *us,* I mean all of *us*, without exception. Some people find this incredibly difficult to grasp, comprehend or even believe, just like the older son. Yet when all is said and done, we do not own God, he does not belong to us, he is not our property, but he is *Our Father,* and he loves *us* all more than we could ever know.

Nine:

God or Money?

Luke 16:1-13

'Time to choose'

Then Jesus said to the disciples, "There was a rich man who had a manager, and charges were brought to him that this man was squandering his property. So, he summoned him and said to him, 'What is this that I hear about you? Give me an accounting of your management because you cannot be my manager any longer.' Then the manager said to himself, 'What will I do now that my master is taking the position away from me? I am not strong enough to dig, and I am ashamed to beg. I have decided what to do so that, when I am dismissed as manager, people may welcome me into their homes.' So, summoning his master's debtors one by one, he asked the first, 'How much do you owe my master?' He answered, 'A hundred jugs of olive oil.' He said to him, 'Take your bill, sit down quickly, and make it fifty.' Then he asked another, 'And how much do you owe?' He replied, 'A hundred containers of wheat.' He said to him, 'Take your bill and make it eighty.' And his master commended the dishonest manager because he had acted shrewdly; for the children of this age are more shrewd in dealing with their own generation than are the children of light. And I tell you, make friends for yourselves by means of dishonest wealth so that when it is gone, they may welcome you into the eternal homes.

"Whoever is faithful in a very little is faithful also in much; and whoever is dishonest in a very little is dishonest also in much. If then you have not been faithful with the dishonest wealth, who will entrust to you the true riches? And if you have not been faithful with what belongs to another, who will give you what is your own? No slave can serve two masters; for a slave will either hate the one and love the other or be devoted to the one and despise the other. You cannot serve God and wealth.

At the time in which Jesus lived money and riches were believed to be a blessing sent from God. Thus, the more wealth you had, then the greater God's favour rested on you. Of course, the only problem with this is that the reverse was also true consigning the poor, once again, to the margins of society. There are, however, many people today who also believe this is true calling it the *Gospel of prosperity*. But how does this approach to God and life square up to the teaching of Jesus?

Growing up in Galilee Jesus would have been all too familiar with the sharp divisions which existed within society. On the one hand there were the rich and powerful landowners who could build up their own personal wealth, whilst on the other there were the subsistent peasant farmers who scratched a living from rented land and were lucky to possess a few copper coins of their own. This made a deep impression on Jesus as he journeyed around the foothills of Galilee and began to reflect on the kind of society, promoted by the religious leaders of the day, who supported the status quo. It is important to keep in mind that Jesus himself was not unlike the peasants he spent so much time with. He owned no land, had no fixed employment and as far as we know possessed no personal wealth. This meant that he was free to speak his mind when it came to God's justice in support of the poor but equally it undermined his teaching credibility in the eyes of the religious leaders such as the Pharisees.

There can be little doubt that Jesus took the side of the poor and those on the margins of society when talking about God's justice but when it comes specifically to money and personal wealth, periodically, he goes into a lot more detail. Jesus never hints at what we have already referred to as the *Gospel of prosperity* but instead equates the accumulation of personal wealth with unfairness and injustice. How then does he come to such a conclusion? There appears to be two answers to this question, firstly such wealth has very often been gained through exploitation of the poor and secondly once amassed it is not used to relieve suffering. This then leaves those who have built up such wealth and fortunes with personal dilemmas, what are they to do? Or putting it more appropriately what are we to do?

The parable gives us an insight into how to answer this question for ourselves when Jesus says, *'I tell you, use worldly wealth to gain friends for yourselves so that when it is gone, you will be welcomed into eternal dwellings.'* At first sight this seems to contradict Jesus's stance on the accumulation of personal wealth, but we need to reflect a little deeper on the point he is getting at. Let us assume that the wealth in question has, as a matter of fact, been raised through the exploitation of the poor, therefore it is tainted. Jesus now challenges the person involved to use the money for good through helping those in need. In this way you will win their friendship and so at the time of death, when personal wealth becomes irrelevant, you will be welcomed into the Father's house. This sounds a bit like money laundering from a gangster film whereby money earned through ill-gotten gains is made clean by *'washing'* it through legitimate means. Is this what Jesus is really saying? In one sense it is, in so far as, he is telling us that if you have gained money in the wrong way, it is not too late. You can still use it, *'tainted as it is,'* to do good. This is a sobering message for the times in which we live because the world and indeed society is as divided today between the rich and the poor as it ever was. Indeed, we are all tempted to justify our personal wealth by arguing that we have earned it but Jesus challenges us to question our motives and not turn our backs on those most in need.

This kind of message did not go down well with religious leaders, of the day, like the Pharisees because they taught the opposite and, as a result, despised the poor and taught others to do the same. Jesus was treated by them with scorn and derision not only because of his message but also because of where he came from, Nazareth in Galilee. Hence, they dismissed his teaching about money because for them the only authentic way to follow God was by keeping his Law and wealth was a sure sign that this was being done.

Yet we are left with a clear and consistent message delivered time and time again by Jesus, that those who have amassed wealth have a responsibility to help people less fortunate than themselves. This, in fact, is not an optional extra but a core teaching of Jesus, which in many ways is designed to make us feel uncomfortable. Those of us who call ourselves Christian, therefore, must reflect on our consciences and guided by the grace of the Holy Spirit and directly by the words of Jesus himself, discern not only how we accumulate our wealth but how we share it with those less fortunate than ourselves. Nowhere is this more important than in the institutional church itself which is called not to live according to the values of the world but according to the values of the Kingdom of Heaven. To this end, the church must practice what it preaches if it is to be true to its Lord and Master. Thus, if the church and indeed Christianity is to speak to a world increasingly obsessed with amassing personal fortunes then it must do so by offering an alternative which conforms directly to what Jesus said himself, *'No servant can serve two masters. Either he will hate one and love the other, or he will be devoted to one and despise the other. You cannot serve both God and money.'* So, when all is said and done Jesus confronts all those who would follow him with the simple choice, God or money?

Ten:

Lazarus

Luke 16:19-31

'Can you see me?'

"There was a rich man who was dressed in purple and fine linen and who feasted sumptuously every day. And at his gate lay a poor man named Lazarus, covered with sores, who longed to satisfy his hunger with what fell from the rich man's table; even the dogs would come and lick his sores. The poor man died and was carried away by the angels to be with Abraham. The rich man also died and was buried. In Hades, where he was being tormented, he looked up and saw Abraham far away with Lazarus by his side. He called out, 'Father Abraham, have mercy on me, and send Lazarus to dip the tip of his finger in water and cool my tongue; for I am in agony in these flames.' But Abraham said, 'Child, remember that during your lifetime you received your good things, and Lazarus in like manner evil things; but now he is comforted here, and you are in agony. Besides all this, between you and us a great chasm has been fixed, so that those who might want to pass from here to you cannot do so, and no one can cross from there to us.' He said, 'Then, father, I beg you to send him to my father's house - for I have five brothers - that he may warn them, so that they will not also come into this place of torment.' Abraham replied, 'They have Moses and the prophets; they should listen to them.' He said, 'No, Father Abraham; but if someone goes to them from the dead, they will repent.' He said to him, 'If they do not listen to Moses and the prophets, neither will they be convinced even if someone rises from the dead.'"

There are no ambiguities in the parables of Jesus in so far as they confront us with the reality of God whilst, at the same time, challenging us to reflect on what that means for our own lives of faith today. Time and time again, Jesus makes something abundantly clear, that the way we live and behave now matters. Ultimately, only lives of mercy, compassion, forgiveness, and love can reflect anything of the nature and being of God. Indeed, what matters more than anything else is the way in which each of us responds to those who suffer. After all, Jesus spent most of his ministry with those who were rejected, despised, unwanted and unloved, even by their own religious leaders.

With this in mind, we can now approach our parable. To begin with note the huge contrast between the two central characters, not unlike that which exists between the rich and the poor today. The rich man dresses in fine purple, the dye for which would have been extremely expensive and is an obvious display of his status for all to see. Thus, he is a man of extreme wealth living a luxurious and comfortable life in every possible way. The passage suggests he is also obsessed with himself, yet he has no name and lacks the one central ingredient required to be open to God and all those who suffer, compassion.

Now we come to the second character, in the parable, found at the rich man's gate. He is poor, hungry, and covered in sores. Perhaps, he is without hope as no one ever comes to his aid except the dogs who, on occasion, come and lick his sores. Yet he has something the rich man does not have; a name and it is Lazarus. This is something we can easily miss but names were important in the ancient world because they established belonging and the meaning of Lazarus comes from Eliezer and means, *'God is my help.'* In the poor man's name, however, we are given a clue as to where Jesus is taking us in the parable.

Both men die but their fortunes are now reversed. The rich man finds himself in hell whilst Lazarus is carried by an angel to Abraham. Here Jesus is making the point that in death God and God alone has the final say. Yet what is really being said here and how is it related to what Jesus has said previously; *'You cannot serve both God and money?'* The way we live and behave now matters and this is the point of the parable. The rich man enjoyed his life and his wealth, though how he achieved his riches is never explained. All we do know, is that either, he never saw, or deliberately chose to ignore, the plight of Lazarus. Where was his compassion? Where was his mercy? Where was his concern for someone less fortunate than himself? He treated Lazarus as if he did not exist and, in the end, that mattered to God a fact Jesus makes abundantly clear. So, what we do and how we behave in this life matters.

At the core of any Christian's being, if we are to be authentic witnesses to Jesus, is compassion, which means action, which means doing something, which means not being indifferent to the cries of the poor and needy. A Christian can never be apathetic in responding to those in need as it is incompatible with the Gospel of Jesus Christ. Our hearts must always be open to the poor, the sick, the dying, those in prison and all those feeling rejected, despised, unwanted and unloved, as this is the way of Christ. Following him is a call to action to make the world in which we live a better place by responding to all forms of suffering. The way of Jesus is to become ever more sensitive to the plight of the sorrowful and to do whatever we can to ease their pain. What better way is there for the church of Jesus Christ to be in the world but not of the world? What better example could there be of bearing witness to faith in Christ than to be on the side of people in need? As the church seeks to explore new ways of responding to the challenges of the modern world, perhaps there can be no better way than conforming itself to the heart of Jesus, which reflects the compassionate Father he came to reveal.

There is no option, for the Christian, to ignore the pleas of the modern-day Lazarus. We cannot close our eyes and simply be indifferent nor can we gather in our churches and worship God without accepting our obligation to recognise and serve Christ in all those who suffer. Because if we do, if we choose to walk by on the other side of the road, ignoring the cries of the poor, we are, in fact, refusing to look into the pleading eyes of Jesus himself, never noticing his outstretched hand in supplication. This truth is what Jesus invites his church and all his followers to bear witness to and live, because in so doing, God speaks.

Eleven:

The Mustard Seed

Luke 17:5-10

'Lord, increase our faith'

The apostles said to the Lord, "Increase our faith!" The Lord replied, "If you had faith the size of a mustard seed, you could say to this mulberry tree, 'Be uprooted and planted in the sea,' and it would obey you.

"Who among you would say to your slave who has just come in from ploughing or tending sheep in the field, 'Come here at once and take your place at the table'? Would you not rather say to him, 'Prepare supper for me, put on your apron and serve me while I eat and drink; later you may eat and drink'? Do you thank the slave for doing what was commanded? So, you also, when you have done all that you were ordered to do, say, 'We are worthless slaves; we have done only what we ought to have done!'"

Perhaps the disciples had been discussing things between themselves, but they approach Jesus and ask him to increase their faith. Did they feel inadequate, or did they simply realise, collectively, that their faith, in him, was not strong enough? On the other hand, however, did they just fail to understand what faith in him really meant? Jesus's response is to describe faith in terms of a mustard seed one of the smallest seeds of all, yet one which grows, nevertheless, into the tallest of all plants. What are we to make of this parable?

My three previous books have concentrated on the birth, death and finally the resurrection of Jesus. If they have taught me anything it is that faith in Christ must come first, above all other things. This may sound obvious, but is it? I remember once, a young girl in a primary school, so she would have been about ten years old, asked me a challenging question, *'If Jesus came to change everything, why is everything still the same?'* Since then, I have come to the conclusion that the only way to answer this question is by turning to Christ and asking him to, *'increase our faith.'*

In the life of Jesus, we see perfectly revealed the nature and being of God and are invited to conform our lives to that of his. Jesus consistently teaches and reveals the God of mercy, compassion, forgiveness, and love. This then is how we must live our lives too, but this is only possible when we have faith in Christ hence, we must constantly ask him to, *'increase our faith.'* I have always been comforted by the words of Saint Augustine of Hippo who said something along the lines of, *the further we move away from the light the darker it gets, the further we move away from the fire the colder we become.* Jesus is, of course, the source of both the light and the warmth and in these words of Augustine we are being urged to stay close to him. The more distant we are from Jesus the less compassionate, merciful, forgiving and loving we become. As a result, the key to everything is faith in Christ, so we can ask again, *'increase our faith.'*

There are times in our own lives of faith and that of the church when we can forget this. How is that possible you might ask, to forget Jesus? Simply because other things appear to take on a higher degree of importance, but it is a grave mistake. You see the very essence of Christianity is believing in a person, Jesus Christ and that he is the Son of God. Not in doctrines, or laws or dogma or theology as important as all these things are but having faith in Christ, this is what really matters. Devoting time to developing a personal relationship with him, staying close to him, conforming our lives to his, allowing him to touch our hearts, these are the things which really matter. Yet if this is to happen, we need to recognise and admit that we need him, hence we must be able to say, *'Lord, increase our faith.'*

When that girl asked me that question all those years ago, what she really wanted to know is, why are people not more like Jesus? Why is the world not a better place? Where is all that mercy, compassion, forgiveness and love so abundantly obvious in his life, not as clear in those who follow him today? Is it possible that somehow, we have lost faith in Jesus and put our trust in other things? That faith, even the size of a mustard seed, is too hard and too demanding given the harsh world in which we live? If this is true, then what is the answer, what do we have to do? We have to say again, with open hearts, *'increase our faith.'* In making this request, however, we must believe that only in Christ can the answers be found and only by walking in his footsteps can we find the way forward, the way back to the light and the source of the warmth.

Jesus invites his disciples and in turn us to place all our hope and all our trust in him. Indeed, it is on the strength of this relationship that everything else depends. Thus, we must rediscover that this is both our own great treasure and that of the church, which is of course faith in Jesus Christ. Only such faith will enable us to walk in his footsteps by living lives devoted to mercy, compassion, forgiveness, and love. If we are not doing this then something has gone seriously wrong and we have lost our way, only to find ourselves cold and in the darkness. Perhaps, this is the image the young girl who asked me the question earlier had of Christianity and of the church and how sad is that. The only way back is, once again, to turn to the Lord and ask him to, *'increase our faith.'*

What that young girl was looking for when she asked me her question was a difference in the world. She wanted to see a more compassionate, merciful, forgiving, and loving humanity. Surely this is what following Jesus is all about? In essence, Jesus reduced his whole teaching to two commandments, loving God and loving neighbour and his parables bear witness to this. Those who would walk in his footsteps are invited to do the same by making the world in which we live a better place for all people. If this is not the case then we need to plead again, *'increase our faith.'*

The answer always must be to return to Christ because for Christianity he is the source of everything and only he can provide the kind of faith we need to be part of his mission to transform the world. Others, including the girl who asked the question earlier, must be able to clearly see his life alive in us. Nothing should distract us from living lives devoted to mercy, compassion, forgiveness, and love. And when the going gets tough and the shadow of the cross threatens to overwhelm us that is when we need to turn to him again and ask, *'increase our faith.'*

If we can do this, even when it is by our fingertips and we are barely hanging on, then Jesus makes something abundantly clear that by virtue of his resurrection from the dead he shares his very life with us. It is this *'Good News'* which he invites us to share with others and all we need to do that is have faith, the size of a mustard seed.

Twelve:

God's Justice

Luke 18:1-8

'I sent you!'

Then Jesus told them a parable about their need to pray always and not to lose heart. He said, "In a certain city there was a judge who neither feared God nor had respect for people. In that city there was a widow who kept coming to him and saying, 'Grant me justice against my opponent.' For a while he refused; but later he said to himself, 'Though I have no fear of God and no respect for anyone, yet because this widow keeps bothering me, I will grant her justice, so that she may not wear me out by continually coming.'" And the Lord said, "Listen to what the unjust judge says. And will not God grant justice to his chosen ones who cry to him day and night? Will he delay long in helping them? I tell you; he will quickly grant justice to them. And yet, when the Son of Man comes, will he find faith on earth?"

Before you read what I have to say about this parable read it through, carefully, for yourself first and then write down what you think it means. Afterwards you can compare our two conclusions because this is one of those parables which can be interpreted in several different ways. The style of my reflections, you may have already gathered, is to discern and reflect upon what Jesus is inviting us to do if we are to be authentic witnesses to his Gospel in the world today. As a result, it will come as no surprise to learn that I will be doing the exact same thing with the parable in question.

Wherever I go, sooner or later, I end up being asked the same question, *'why doesn't God do something about the state of the world?'* The answer I give tends to be, *'he has, he sent you, so what are you doing?'* Straight away this puts most people on the back foot because it challenges them to provide a credible answer. *So, what would you say? How would you answer this question? See what I mean?*

In the parable we have a widow, a woman without the help and support of her husband or children. As a result, she would have been helpless in the world in which she lived and therefore open to exploitation. So, she approaches a judge who appears to care nothing for her plight and is without the necessary ingredient needed, according to Jesus, to reflect something of the nature of God, compassion. What the widow asks for is justice, something she repeats over and over again but her refrain falls on deaf ears. I wonder how many people in the world right now are crying out to God asking for justice. How many of us hear their pleading?

Two features can now be identified in this parable which are equally applicable to the world of today. Firstly, how hard the heart of the judge is and secondly, the apparent silence of God. This in turn should now prompt us to ask, *'how hard are our hearts,'* to those who cry out for justice and *'what are we doing about it?'* And equally, can those who cry out see God responding in and through his people? I made the point earlier that in one of my previous books, *'Sharing in the Life of God – A Journey into the Real Meaning of Easter,'* what defines our humanity, in my opinion, is how we respond to suffering. Yet, this is something which could also be equally applied to the church. That those who purport to follow Christ should be more like him, which in essence, means being compassionate.

Such compassion, inevitably, should make us more aware of and, therefore, more sensitive to all those who cry out for justice in the world. Are not such people making a direct plea to the heart of their Father and Our Father? And did this loving and compassionate Father not send us? And, therefore, is he not entitled to ask of us, *'what are you doing?'* In this way the parable can be seen, as a direct challenge to all those who would associate themselves with Jesus, in any way, to listen to and respond to the cries of all victims of injustice. It is not enough just to pray and worship, as important as these may be, the Father expects more of us than that. We cannot turn our backs on the victims of injustice whilst at the same time associating our lives of faith with Jesus Christ. All over the world right now people are crying out for justice and experiencing, in response, hardness of heart and silence. This is not the way of Jesus Christ nor of those who follow him. The only way for the church and all those who call themselves Christian to respond to such cries is with the compassion of Jesus, which in turn reveals the face of the Father. In this way God is not silent because he hears the cries of his people and he sends us.

Now compare your understanding of the parable with what I have written, what conclusions did you come to? The important thing to keep in mind is that the parables very often challenge us, they shake us up by encouraging us to examine and re-evaluate our lives of faith. They can even make us feel uncomfortable and disturb us but do not worry when that happens because it is a sure sign that grace is at work and that the parable is, in fact, doing exactly what Jesus intended it to do.

Thirteen:

The Humble will be Exalted

Luke 18:9-14

'God and me'

He also told this parable to some who trusted in themselves that they were righteous and regarded others with contempt: "Two men went up to the temple to pray, one a Pharisee and the other a tax collector. The Pharisee, standing by himself, was praying thus, 'God, I thank you that I am not like other people: thieves, rogues, adulterers, or even like this tax collector. I fast twice a week; I give a tenth of all my income.' But the tax collector, standing far off, would not even look up to heaven, but was beating his breast and saying, 'God, be merciful to me, a sinner!' I tell you; this man went down to his home justified rather than the other; for all who exalt themselves will be humbled, but all who humble themselves will be exalted."

As we work our way through the parables of Jesus, we must be courageous enough to apply their meaning to ourselves and our own lives of faith. This will not be easy because it is not meant to be, and the pre-requisite is personal honesty. In this parable there are two principal characters, but it is clear from Luke's point of view that Jesus is addressing primarily those who see themselves as more righteous than those they looked down on. So, both characters make their way to the temple to pray, what happens next is an insight into how we should relate to God and comes to us directly from Jesus himself.

The Pharisee is obviously a man of deep faith, not only teaching the Law of God but keeping it. Once inside the temple he clearly knows what, he believes, is expected of him. He is a man of confidence and stands with his head held high before God. Yet Jesus wants us to learn something about how this man now prays and, therefore, what his relationship with God is like. The first thing to notice is that he glorifies himself rather than God and boasts about all the good he has done. Perhaps he feels justified before God because he knows he is, in fact, better than everyone else. But is this prayer? He never recognises the glory of God or how great God is compared to him. There are no concessions to the great mystery of God. Instead, there is confusion as to where true greatness lies. He asks God for nothing and prays for no one and we are left to conclude that this Pharisee does not need God because he has done everything for himself. We might even say he is self-absorbed or obsessed with himself. But is this prayer and is this the kind of relationship Jesus invites us to have with our heavenly Father?

We now come to the second character in the parable, the tax collector and reflect on how he prays in the temple compared to that of the Pharisee. The first thing to note is that he is all too aware of his despised occupation as a tax collector and that to many people he is not welcome in God's house at all. Hence, he knows that he is a sinner and despised by his fellow Jews as he prays, *'God, have mercy on me a sinner.'*

Unlike the Pharisee, the tax collector has nothing to exhort over or boast about because he lacks anything worthy to offer God. Yet he recognises that he has a great need, to be loved and forgiven by his heavenly Father. In other words, what he desires more than anything else, is the mercy of God. Here Jesus wants us to recognise the honesty and sincerity of the prayer offered by the tax collector. He may have lost his way in life but recognises that only God can bring him back.

Jesus in this parable is urging us to develop the right attitude towards God in our lives of faith and prayer. The tax collector shows us the way because he recognises how much he needs God, whilst the Pharisee, on the other hand, does not need God at all because he can do everything for himself. One attitude puts us on the right path leading us to the Father, the other takes us in the opposite direction. Listen again to the words of the tax collector, *'God, have mercy on me, a sinner,'* because it tells us all we need to know, which is that first and foremost we need God. None of us are perfect and all goodness owes its origin to God. It is our need to recognise this and to approach our Father with contrite hearts in need of his mercy, which will draw us ever closer to his heart.

As the two characters enter the temple, they do so with two completely different attitudes towards God. For the Pharisee faith is a matter of following the Law of God and doing this will make him both righteous and good. Indeed, the more faithful and obedient to the Law he is, the greater his status before others and the more important he becomes. As a result, he needs nothing because in his own minds eye he is, in fact, perfect. The tax collector on the other hand fulfils Jesus's expectations of what it means to be close to God. In the depths of his heart, he has asked for and received the mercy, forgiveness, and love that only his Father could give. Yet, at the same time he has boasted about nothing and condemned no one. This is the attitude Jesus encourages us to develop in our relationship with God. It is not easy because it demands total honesty, but it frees us from all false images of God and self, leaving us with a relationship of dependency but in the right way. What Jesus is telling us here, therefore, is that we must recognise our need for God's mercy, forgiveness, and love because only that will set us free to love others in the same way that he loves us.

Life, Faith, and the Parables – some final thoughts

In this final section I am going to reflect on what I have learned, personally, by reflecting on the parables of Jesus and how this affects the way in which I live out my own faith on a day-to-day basis. We can, of course, no longer see Jesus in the flesh but through the grace of his Holy Spirit he is still with us, alive and active, in both the world and in our own lives. His words, however, have special significance because it is through them that he reveals the will of his Father. The sacred scriptures have kept these words alive for over two millennia offering us hope and the key as to how we are to live our lives of faith today. I often find that there is a longing in my own heart to see Jesus face to face and my faith tells me that one day this will happen but until then I have learned to treasure his words in my heart and allow them to shape the course of my life.

Hence the parables tell me that life is not meaningless but has a purpose and if we live our lives in accordance with their teaching we are, in fact, part of a process which will eventually lead to the salvation of the whole world. This means, ultimately, that things will not be as they are now forever. War, injustice, poverty, persecution, and inequality will all eventually come to an end. One day the true potential for humanity will be realised when his kingdom of justice and peace for all will be established. Until that day comes, we have a mission given to us by Christ himself and that is to live our lives in accordance with his will.

When I look around the world today, however, I am very often confronted with the misery of suffering humanity. I cannot believe that God is indifferent to this, but the parables tell me that there is, in fact, something I can do, which is everything within my power to relieve the suffering, misery and pain of others. Eventually God himself will intervene wiping the tears away from the faces of all those who suffer but until then it is up to me to do whatever I can to give others a foretaste of the compassion of Christ. The parables have taught me that every act of human kindness serves as an anticipation or foretaste of what life will be like when all those who suffer meet Jesus face to face because then, *'The first shall be last and the last shall be first.'* On that day, all that such people have been denied in this world will be granted to them and they will know the comfort, consolation, and well-being that only God can give.

The parables have taught me that the values of the Kingdom of Heaven are not the same as the values of the world. Shining through the words of Jesus we begin to understand not only what God is like but how he invites us to live our lives by being merciful, compassionate, forgiving, and loving. In this way the parables have helped me seek the gentleness and tenderness of Christ in others. Of course, as I have already said, I long to see his face but until that day finally comes, he has invited me to seek him in others, especially in those who suffer. The world often turns its back on the weak and the powerless, but it is in them that, perhaps, God is to be most acutely found. He will never forget his people and one day he will reach out to each and every single one of them and say, *'Come with me, see I did not forget you.'* Similarly, there are many people all over the world who, largely unknown, dedicate their lives to relieving the pain, misery and suffering of others. In the same way, they will not be forgotten by the Lord because they are people who, literally, make the parables of Jesus live.

The one great treasure I have learnt from the parables is that God loves all people, unconditionally, and that we are called simply to do the same. In my experience many people do this anonymously and seek no reward and yet in them I see clearly, right before my very eyes, the words of those same parables, live. Thus, when it comes to the church, the parables for me make something abundantly clear that its mission is to humanity and its message is that in and through his Son, God loves all people.

The parables have also taught me that everything is given as a free gift. We do not have to earn God's love because it is simply given. The great sadness then is, perhaps, our inability to grasp this great truth of our faith. In the parable of the *Lost Son*, the younger brother eventually had to realise this for himself but in truth his father never stopped loving him. In the parable of the *Labourers in the Vineyard* those who came first had to learn that God's love is given in equal measure to all. Whilst in the parable of the *Good Samaritan* compassion was given as a free gift even to an enemy. The world like the older brother in the *Lost Son* wants to shout out, *'this is not fair,'* but it is the way of God and he invites it to be our way too.

The final thing I want to add is something I have said and reflected upon before in the pages of this book and it draws my attention back to the face of Jesus, whilst at the same time making me feel incredibly humble. Until he returns or on the day, we meet him face to face in heaven Christ charges us with giving others a foretaste of him, of his compassion, of his mercy, of his forgiveness and ultimately of his love. How are we to do this? Well, that is where the parables come in.

I thank you for taking the time to read this book, I hope that in some small way it has served to draw you closer to Our Lord.

God Bless

Thank You

To write a book like this, requires time alone with God listening and responding to the promptings of the Holy Spirit. For this reason, I often spent many hours in my office, at home, tapping away at the keyboard on my computer, whilst my wife waited patiently downstairs. Therefore, the first person I need to thank in the writing of this book is my wife Pam not only for putting up with me but also for constantly believing in the importance of what God has invited me to do. Secondly, I thank my family but especially my three sons, Lance, Thomas, and James who never seem to let me off the hook when it comes to trying to live a life of honesty, decency, and integrity – thanks guys! I also want to express my gratitude to the people, parish, and school of Our Lady of the Wayside where my faith and love of God, in Christ, over time, has been both enriched and deepened. Particularly I want to thank Creina Hearn for her constant support in all my writing projects and Shirley Hanlon for planting the seed in my mind out of which grew this very book; now there is a parable if there ever was one! I would also like to thank His Grace the Archbishop of Birmingham, Bernard Longley, for his support and for agreeing to write the foreword, it is truly humbling. And then there is Barney who died on 10th November 2021, thank you for your friendship and loyalty, I hope that one day we can meet again. Finally, I would like to thank you, the reader for taking the time to read this book. I hope that, in some small way, it has helped you grow in your understanding of God and his son Jesus Christ. After all, it was for you that this book was written in the first place.

About the Author

Sean Loone is a Roman Catholic Deacon working in the Archdiocese of Birmingham. He has spent much of his career teaching in a variety of schools and colleges combining this with lecturing part-time at Saint Mary's College Oscott, the seminary for the Archdiocese. Currently he acts as chaplain and Religious Education advisor to a number of academic establishments including Our Lady of the Wayside, his home parish, where he is also the Catholic Life governor. His academic interests, on which he has published many articles, include Biblical studies and Christology. His most recent publication was a book called, *'Servants of the Word – The Gospel of Christ and the Call to Discipleship.'* He also has extensive pastoral and sacramental experience combining this with a ministry dedicated to proclaiming God's word through both preaching and teaching the scriptures. He is married with three sons and is currently working on a new project, which aims, this time, to explore the meaning of Advent and Christmas for people today.

By the Same Author

'Born for Us – A Journey into the Real Meaning of Christmas'
Available from ALIVE Publishing (2019)

'Only in the Crucified Christ – Questions and Answers on Faith, Hope and Love'
Available from Amazon (2020) - All profits to CAFOD

'Sharing in the Life of God – A Journey into the Real Meaning of Easter'
Available from Amazon (2021) – All profits to the Father Mahony Memorial Trust

'Servants of the Word – The Gospel of Christ and the Call to Discipleship'
Available from Amazon (2021) – All profits to Father Hudson's Care

'Get you up to a high mountain,
O Zion, herald of *good news*;
lift up your voice with strength,
O Jerusalem, herald of *good news*,
lift it up, fear not;
say to the cities of Judah,
"Behold your God!"
Behold, the Lord GOD comes with might.'

(Isaiah 40:9-10)

'The grass withers, the flower fades,
but the word of God remains for ever'

(Isaiah 40:8)

'Heaven and Earth will pass away,
but my words will never pass away'

(Mark 13:31)

Available worldwide from Amazon

_____

Michael Terence
Publishing

www.mtp.agency

www.facebook.com/mtp.agency

@mtp_agency

Printed in Great Britain
by Amazon

79992388R00082